PENGUIN PASSNOTES

WILLIAM SHAKESPEARE

Macbeth

S. H. COOTE M.A., PH.D.

PENGUIN BOOKS

Penguin Books Ltd, Harmondsworth, Middlesex, England
Viking Penguin Inc., 40 West 23rd Street, New York, New York 10010, U.S.A.
Penguin Books Australia Ltd, Ringwood, Victoria, Australia
Penguin Books Canada Ltd, 2801 John Street, Markham, Ontario, Canada L3R 1B4
Penguin Books (N.Z.) Ltd, 182–190 Wairau Road, Auckland 10, New Zealand

First published 1984
Reprinted 1984, 1986, 1987 (twice)

Made and printed in Great Britain by
Richard Clay Ltd, Bungay, Suffolk
Filmset in Monophoto Ehrhardt

*The publishers are grateful to the following Examination Boards for
permission to reproduce questions from examination papers used in
individual titles in the Passnotes series:*

*Associated Examining Board, University of Cambridge Local Examinations
Syndicate, Joint Matriculation Board, University of London School
Examination Department, Oxford and Cambridge Schools Examination
Board, University of Oxford Delegacy of Local Examinations.*

*The Examination Boards accept no responsibility whatsoever for the
accuracy or method of working in any suggested answers given as models.*

PENGUIN PASSNOTES

Macbeth

Dr Stephen Coote was educated at Cambridge and London
University. He was Director of Studies and Head of English
at tutorial colleges in London and Oxford. He has written a
number of other guides in the Passnotes series including:
Wuthering Heights, Twelfth Night and *Chaucer: The Prologue
to the Canterbury Tales*.

Contents

To the Student

This book is designed to help you with your O-level or C.S.E. English Literature examinations. It contains an introduction to the play, analysis of scenes and characters, and a commentary on some of the issues raised by the play. Line references are to the New Penguin Shakespeare, edited by G. K. Hunter.

When you use this book remember that it is no more than an aid to your study. It will help you find passages quickly and perhaps give you some ideas for essays. But remember: *This book is not a substitute for reading the play and it is your response and your knowledge that matter.* These are the things the examiners are looking for, and they are also the things that will give you the most pleasure. Show your knowledge and appreciation to the examiner, and show them clearly.

Introduction: Background to Macbeth

Macbeth is one of the most dramatic plays ever written. It opens with witches, encompasses the murder of a king and the appearance of a ghost, and ends in madness, despair and death. Every moment of it is full of action and there is in it some of the most powerful poetry in the English language.

Shakespeare wrote the play for performance some time in 1606. He was by then the most successful dramatist in the country, patronized by James I, for whom the play was written.

This tells us a great deal. James was Scottish and was passionately interested both in witchcraft and in the nature of kingship. He also enjoyed spectacular theatre. *Macbeth* fulfils all these requirements. It has never really lost its popularity since it was first performed.

In the play we see a great man, a strong man, destroyed by submitting to forces of evil over which he has no control. We watch him as he moves from being a loyal subject to becoming a traitor and a cruel tyrant. We see his wife appear as the very personification of evil, only to crack under the force of conscience and become a mad wraith.

But why is the play a tragedy? Why are we moved by the sight of a hero transformed into a devil? How is it that a man who indulges in murder does not come across to us simply as a monster: a Stalin or a Hitler? The reason lies in the fact that Macbeth realizes the enormity of his crimes and understands why he suffers so desperately. It is not only the good man who is aware of the nature of goodness. By being cut off from them, Macbeth knows what goodness, peace and security are. It is the power of Shakespeare's poetry, difficult though it often is, which conveys to us Macbeth's heroic suffering. In this lies his true status as a tragic hero: he moves both our pity and our terror.

Synopsis

Amid thunder and lightning three Witches appear. They know that a battle is being fought and they agree to meet again after it, this time on the heath where they will encounter Macbeth. This scene sets the play's mood of storm, magic and evil power.

We move to where King Duncan and his court are camped near the scene of battle (I, ii). A wounded Captain describes how fierce the battle was. A part of the rebel forces, led by Macdonwald, were on the point of victory when Macbeth carved his way through them, tore Macdonwald in half with his sword and fixed his head on the battlements. We have not seen Macbeth yet, although we know him to be brave, bloody and loyal to his king. This great soldier, having destroyed part of the enemy force, now furiously vanquishes the Norwegians led by the Thane of Cawdor. Ross and Angus report this second victory to King Duncan, who is so delighted by Macbeth's valour that he creates him Thane of Cawdor in place of the traitor who is to be summarily executed. This is a fit reward for a loyal man of action.

The Witches reappear, again accompanied by thunder (I, iii). They describe where they have been and what they have been doing. The First Witch, in revenge for being refused a chestnut by a sailor's wife, tells how she will torture him. We are made more fully aware of the Witches' evil. Drum-beats announce the arrival of Macbeth, and the Witches dance to summon up their magic.

Macbeth and Banquo enter. Suddenly they see the Witches. Banquo questions them. They do not answer, but when Macbeth speaks to them they greet him as the Thane of Glamis (which he is), Thane of Cawdor (which the King, though Macbeth does not know it, has just made him) and as future king. Macbeth is amazed but says nothing. Banquo questions the Witches about his own future, but they answer in riddles. Macbeth, who has been silent all this while, asks the Witches to be more explicit, but they vanish. Almost immediately, Ross and Angus enter to tell Macbeth he has been made the Thane of Cawdor. The first of the Witches' prophecies has instantly come true. As Angus is praising him, Macbeth mutters that even better things are to come. Banquo hints that the Witches may be dangerous.

The first of Macbeth's soliloquies follows. The great man of action is plunged into confused thought. The idea of murdering Duncan appals him: but he *has* imagined it. For the moment he will leave things to chance. The scene ends with the sense of Macbeth as a man with something evil on his mind.

Malcolm, the King's son, describes the noble death of the traitor Cawdor (I, iv). Duncan comments that one can never judge a man by his looks. At this moment Macbeth enters. Duncan praises him, trusting him absolutely, and Macbeth (who is not yet a traitor in deed though already in thought) replies that he has done no more than a loyal subject should. He defines loyalty. Duncan then commends Banquo for his labours and, now that he seems safe from traitors, looks to the future and declares Malcolm his heir. In an aside, Macbeth plunges into his second major soliloquy. Evil ambition is fermenting in his mind, and the new heir is a threat. He wants to *make* the Witches' prophecies come true. He exits. Duncan follows, to spend the night in Macbeth's castle.

We now meet Lady Macbeth (I, v). She is reading the letter in which Macbeth describes his meeting with the Witches. Her own ambition is clear, but she fears that her husband's nature is too kindly to be ruthless and makes up her mind to rouse him to action. When a Messenger announces the imminent arrival of Duncan, a second soliloquy shows her ambition in full flood. She no longer wants to be a natural, motherly woman, but a murderess at one with darkness and evil. When her husband enters she greets him (like the Witches) as Glamis, Cawdor and future king. Macbeth repeats the news that Duncan is coming, and Lady Macbeth, taking matters into her own hands, tells her husband to appear welcoming but to plan evil. He has doubts ('We will speak further . . .'), but Lady Macbeth appears resolute, a woman of iron will.

Duncan arrives (I, vi). He admires the beauty of Macbeth's castle, little knowing that it is soon to become a hell on earth and the place of his own death. Lady Macbeth, full of flattery, leads him in.

We next see Macbeth alone (I, vii). The great warrior and man of action is racked by his conscience. He who can slaughter men in battle cannot bring himself to murder this one man: his king. He is Duncan's host and his vassal. God appoints kings, and a man who assassinates a king assures his own damnation. Macbeth, the man of action, is paralysed. He tries to persuade Lady Macbeth to forget her plan, but she turns on him and calls him an unmanly coward – only by having the courage to murder Duncan will he prove his manhood. She details her plan for the murder and the horrified Macbeth is persuaded. In the first Act he is transformed from hero to traitor.

It is almost midnight and dark in the castle. Macbeth is prowling round and meets Banquo (II, i). They mention the Witches and agree to speak more of them later. Banquo leaves to go to bed. Macbeth dismisses his servant, ordering him to ask Lady Macbeth to 'strike upon the bell' when his drink is ready. This is to be the signal for the murder of Duncan.

Left on his own, the conscience-ridden Macbeth imagines he sees a dagger floating before him. His nerves are overwrought to the point of hallucination. The visionary dagger, reappearing, has blood on it. Macbeth tries to calm himself, but is prey to images of witchcraft, murder and rape. The bell rings, summoning him to Duncan's murder. Ambition has got the better of fear and conscience.

Lady Macbeth enters, slightly drunk (II, ii). Her heroic resolve was just a show. She was to have murdered Duncan, but the sleeping king reminded her of her father and pity made her falter. The grooms at Duncan's door are in a drunken and drugged sleep, and Lady Macbeth has left their daggers beside them for her husband to use in his murder of the King.

Macbeth returns with the bloodstained daggers. He has committed the murder, but at a terrible cost. He and his wife speak nervously to each other. Macbeth is revolted by the blood and terrified because he can no longer pray nor sleep. The murder of the King has cut him off from God and from all peace of mind. Lady Macbeth tells him he is being ridiculous; he must wash the blood from his hands and take the daggers back. If he puts them beside the grooms, it will look as if the grooms killed Duncan in a drunken fury. Macbeth is too afraid to go back, and Lady Macbeth, snatching the daggers from him, returns to the bedroom herself.

There is a loud knocking at the castle gates. We will discover that it comes from Macduff and Lennox, but for the moment it echoes horribly, fearfully and anonymously round the castle. The noise tortures the guilt-stricken Macbeth with fear. Lady Macbeth tries to encourage her suffering husband into putting a convincing face on things – 'Be not lost/So poorly in your thoughts.'

There follows the Porter scene (II, iii). The Porter in his drunkenness imagines himself to be the porter at the gate of hell – in a sense he is. After some comic dialogue, he lets Macduff and Lennox into the castle where they meet Macbeth. Lennox tells him of the terrible storm that raged the previous night. Macduff, who has gone to see Duncan, returns in horror after discovering that Duncan has been murdered. Macbeth leaves to investigate, and Macduff has the alarm bell rung and rouses the castle. The pandemonium that follows summons Lady Macbeth, who feigns ignorance and horror at the news of the murder. Macbeth, in a short but crucial soliloquy, meditates on the murder of Duncan; with this act he has destroyed both his own peace and his reason for living. His life will now be an ever more complex series of lies, violence and desperation. To cover every trace of his crime, he tells Macduff that he killed the grooms who, it is to be thought, murdered the King. He did so, he says, in a fit of confused anguish and loyalty. Lady Macbeth faints and is carried away. Banquo suggests that they all gather to investigate in detail what has happened, but Malcolm and Donalbain, the King's sons, realizing that suspicion may well fall on them (Malcolm, after all, was the heir and is now the rightful king) decide to find safety in England and Ireland respectively.

The murder of the King has its effect on the whole country, and this is demonstrated in Act II Scene iv. Such a murder is unnatural; it goes against the laws of nature. As a result of it, other unnatural events take place which the Old Man describes to Ross. Macduff arrives and tells Ross that it is generally believed that Malcolm and Donalbain bribed the grooms to murder their father and then fled in fear. Macbeth, it seems, has committed the crime without rousing suspicion. He has been named king and has already gone to Scone to be crowned. Macduff, Ross and the Old Man part.

But Banquo has his suspicions. He thinks Macbeth may well have murdered Duncan to become king (III, i) and, remembering the Witches' prophecies to Macbeth, he wonders how their promises to him will be fulfilled. His thoughts are interrupted by the arrival of Macbeth and his wife, who, anxious to win and preserve his good opinion, invite him to a feast. Macbeth questions Banquo closely about the ride he is to take that afternoon. It transpires that Macbeth is deeply suspicious of Banquo. He recognizes his loyalty to true kingship and his bravery. He is also worried by the Witches' promise that it is Banquo's children who will succeed to the crown. If this comes true, then Macbeth has murdered and lost his soul for nothing. In the hope of securing the throne for his descendants, Macbeth has decided to have Banquo murdered. He has hired two ruffians for this purpose. These men he now persuades to the deed.

Lady Macbeth, seemingly so strong at her first entrance, is breaking under the strain of guilt. She knows, however, that she must put a brave face on things and keep up the appearance of unnatural ruthlessness with which she seeks to keep her husband from despair (III, ii). She tries to win him over from his exhausting self-questioning and begs him to seem sociable at the feast that night. He promises, but his despair keeps breaking through. Without saying precisely what he has in mind, he hints to her of the plan for the murder of Banquo. Although his conscience is sorely troubled, Macbeth believes he can make himself secure through further murder.

The murder of Banquo takes place, but his son Fleance escapes (III, iii). This is the boy, of course, from whom a new line of kings will come, kings who trace their descent from Banquo. The Witches' prophecy will be fulfilled, and there is nothing Macbeth can do to prevent this; he is not master of his fate.

We are now shown the promised feast (III, iv). Macbeth welcomes his guests and tries to play the good host. As he does so, the first of the murderers slips in and reports his bungled attempt to kill Banquo and Fleance. Banquo indeed is dead but Macbeth realizes that his security is permanently threatened by Fleance's escape. He is deeply troubled. Again it seems that he has murdered Duncan for nothing. Lady Macbeth reminds Macbeth of his duties to his guests, and he makes an effort to behave as a host should. At this point the entrance of Banquo's ghost, visible only to Macbeth, reduces him to confusion and terror. Not only has he failed to secure his future, but now he is literally haunted by his past. Lady Macbeth first tries to excuse his wild behaviour to the guests, and then rounds on her husband. He cannot be easily silenced, however, and the second appearance of the ghost and Macbeth's subsequent outbursts cause the feast to break up. Lady Macbeth orders the guests from the hall.

Alone and weary, Macbeth and his wife wonder why Macduff failed to come to the feast. This is suspicious. What does Macduff suspect? Macbeth, already becoming the tyrant, tells his wife he has planted spies in the houses of all the Thanes; he intends to go back to the Witches and force the truth from them. He must know what is to happen, yet there is so much blood on his hands the future hardly matters.

We meet the Witches again in Act III Scene v. Just as there is confusion in the kingdom of Scotland, so there is in the kingdom of darkness: Hecate is furious that she has been allowed no part in Macbeth's downfall. She points out that Macbeth wants evil to triumph for his sake, not for theirs. She orders her companions to return the following day so that they can raise visions that will drive Macbeth mad.

Act III Scene vi demonstrates the suspicions that have been aroused in Scotland. Men cannot speak of these suspicions directly, but must live by hints and unanswered questions. Macbeth is clearly thought of as a bloody tyrant. Lennox and an unnamed Lord discuss Malcolm, the legitimate heir. The young man is no longer regarded with suspicion. He is living in England at the court of the holy Edward the Confessor. In order that Scotland's suffering shall end, Macduff has gone to seek him out there and raise a force to reconquer the kingdom. Macbeth, too, is preparing for war.

In a dramatic scene, the Witches prepare their evil charms (IV, i).

Hecate congratulates them, and Macbeth enters. He demands answers to his questions, whatever the cost. The Witches then call up the Apparitions. Macbeth begins to ask the First Apparition a question, but is told by the First Witch that he must not speak but simply listen. The First Apparition, in the form of an armed head, warns Macbeth to beware of Macduff. The Second Apparition, as a bloody child, tells Macbeth he has nothing to fear from a man born of woman. The Third Apparition tells Macbeth he can never be defeated until Birnan Wood marches on his castle at Dunsinane. These last two Apparitions seem to promise Macbeth perfect safety; but he still wants to know whether Banquo's descendants will reign in Scotland. The Witches warn him against pressing this question, but he insists. A visionary procession of eight kings and Banquo appears and illustrates that this prophecy, like all the rest, will indeed come true. In anguish, Macbeth asks if this will really come to pass. Will Banquo's children be kings of Scotland? The Witches refuse to answer. They dance, and vanish.

Lennox enters and Macbeth asks him if he saw the Witches on his way, but it seems they appeared only to Macbeth. Macbeth curses them; when he is told that Macduff has fled to England, confirming the First Apparition's warning, he swears he will wipe out Macduff's whole family. Macbeth has become as crazed as Hecate intended. The hero of the first Act is now a homicidal tyrant.

We next see Lady Macduff and her son (IV, ii). She tells Ross how cruel and foolish her husband was to leave her undefended in Scotland. Ross tries to comfort her, but Lady Macduff firmly believes her husband to be dead. She is a woman alone in the kingdom of a tyrant. Charming, innocent conversation then takes place between Lady Macduff and her son. It is this innocence that Macbeth will wantonly destroy. A Messenger comes to warn Lady Macduff of her danger. It is too late. She and her son face their murderers, who have suddenly come upon them, and are horribly butchered. The insane, ruthless desperation of Macbeth could not be made more clear.

Act IV Scene iii takes place in England, at the court of Edward the Confessor. Malcolm and Macduff bewail the misfortunes of Scotland. Malcolm vows revenge and tries to encourage Macduff, telling him of the troops that have been raised. But Malcolm is a shrewd politician.

wants to test the depth of Macduff's loyalty and does so by pretending that he, the legitimate king, is no better than Macbeth — worse, even. He pretends to be sexually promiscuous, avaricious, and utterly lacking in all the qualities that make a good monarch. Macduff at first excuses him: after all, Malcolm is the rightful king. Eventually he has to confess that Malcolm, as he has described himself, is not only unfit to govern, he is unfit even to live. There is, it seems, no hope for Scotland, and Macduff despairs for her. Malcolm is moved by such patriotism and declares that he is in fact the very opposite of the character he has presented: he is a virgin, a plain dealer, and an honest man. Macduff, confused, is prevented from questioning Malcolm on the false presentation of himself by the entry of Ross and the news of the butchering of his family. He is once again plunged into complete despondency. Malcolm urges him to turn his thoughts to revenge, to use his anger for the good of the country. Malcolm now prepares to lead his army into Scotland.

Lady Macbeth is seen for the last time at the beginning of Act V. She is a broken woman. The character whom we first saw defying her natural instincts and giving every impression of strength has been destroyed by the power of conscience which she thought was of no importance. Her mad speeches (significantly, these are in prose) are pathetic. Watched by a Doctor and her Gentlewoman, she is endlessly reliving fragments of her guilty past: her bloodstained hands, the memory of Banquo, the reluctance of her husband to murder his king. The Doctor confesses that he can do nothing for her. It is her spirit that is sick, not her body. She needs a priest, not a physician.

The English forces, led by Malcolm, are gathering near Birnan Wood (V, ii). They learn that the desperate Macbeth has fortified his castle and some say he is insane. Confident of their power, the army marches on to battle.

Isolated in his castle, Macbeth repeats the prophecies of the Apparitions: no one can harm him till Birnan Wood moves to Dunsinane (V, iii). No man born of woman, he has been told, shall have power over him; why, then, should he worry that his army is deserting him? He turns on the Messenger who brings news of the English advance, and then falls into the deep pessimism that gives him something of nobility in these last scenes. He arms himself, defiant to the end. Since medicine, as he tells the Doctor, cannot cure a sick mind, perhaps fighting can. Ironically the corrupted Macbeth becomes, in his desperation, the soldier and man of action we saw at the start of the play.

Malcolm has the loyalty of his troops to support him (V, iv). He orders his men to camouflage themselves by each bearing a branch from the trees of Birnan Wood as they march. The wood will then appear to be moving. The Witches' prophecies once again come true.

Macbeth remains defiant until he hears the cry of women and is told that his wife is dead (V, v). He then speaks the last and perhaps the greatest of his soliloquies. In Act II, Scene iii, immediately after the discovery of Duncan's murder, he knew that life had become meaningless; now, with great poetry, he expresses his exhausted resignation in the face of what he sees as life's futility. The moving quality of this speech almost redeems him. Immediately after it he is told that Birnan Wood appears to be on the move towards his castle and, with something of the savage nobility of a cornered animal, Macbeth turns to fight.

The English army sound their trumpets and we watch Macbeth fighting a losing battle (V, vi). Challenged by Young Siward, Macbeth kills him. Here was no more than a young man born of woman. But now Macduff is seeking him, spurred by the need for revenge. The castle has surrendered and Macduff forces his way in to find his enemy, whom he challenges. Macbeth has all the fury of a desperate man. He repeats the Apparition's promise of a seemingly charmed life. But Macduff, who has been born by Caesarean section (in other words, not naturally and by a woman's efforts) is here to fulfil the last of the Apparitions' prophecies. After a tremendous struggle he kills Macbeth.

The victorious nobles gather round Malcolm. Siward is told of his son's death, and Ross comforts him by describing Young Siward's valour. The victory is confirmed as Macduff enters with Macbeth's severed head and proclaims Malcolm king. Malcolm, in gratitude for their support, honours his 'thanes and kinsmen' by creating earldoms, for them and, promising to bring peace and order to Scotland, invites them to witness his coronation at Scone.

Scene by Scene Analysis

ACT I SCENE i

Macbeth opens with a vivid impression of evil: the appearance of the three Witches amid thunder and lightning. The impact is a strongly visual one. By amazing his audience with the supernatural before we meet the humans in the play, Shakespeare sets the tone of evil and magic. He convinces us of the Witches' power. We know that their meeting with Macbeth can do him no good. Before we even see him, there is the suggestion that Macbeth is a doomed man, one whom the forces of evil wish to destroy.

The storm in which the Weird Sisters are seen is more than theatrical spectacle. It suggests (as does the storm described by Lennox in Act II Scene iii) the chaotic and elemental power of evil, the very forces of destruction Macbeth will unleash on Scotland.

ACT I SCENE ii

It is important to realize that at the start of the play Macbeth is a hero: a loyal and brave soldier. Scotland is threatened by a rebellion led by Macdonwald. It is very nearly successful. The 'bleeding Captain' describes a ferocious battle between all but equal forces. It is 'brave Macbeth' who saves the day. Sword in hand, he hacks his way through the rebels until he finds their leader and tears him in half. The Macbeth described here is a war machine, a man of blood and action in the service of his king. This impression is heightened as the Captain tells of Macbeth's second assault. Yet a third attack, the final and victorious one, is described by Ross. Macbeth has routed the Norwegians who are now begging for peace. Duncan is delighted. His throne and his country are safe. He orders the death sentence for the treacherous Thane of Cawdor and gives his title to Macbeth. It is a fitting reward for a loyal servant.

But *Macbeth* is a play about illusion: events and people seem to be one thing; they turn out to be another. The loyal Macbeth will become as great a traitor as the man whose title he has now received. He starts as a war machine employed for his country's good, yet this violence will be turned on his king and the people. His victory has brought peace to Scotland, but his tyrannical rule will bring anguish.

Look how vividly Shakespeare's language brings the battle to life: Macbeth's sword 'smoked with bloody execution', Macdonwald is 'unseamed ... from the nave to th' chops'. Macbeth and Banquo are compared to eagles and lions; Macbeth himself is 'Bellona's bridegroom', that is, a warrior fit to wed the goddess of war. Notice, too, how the descriptions of battle concentrate on Macbeth. It is he, in person, who wins the day.

ACT I SCENE iii

When the Witches re-enter, we move from heroic battle to vicious creatures who slaughter pigs or torment sailors. There is nothing heroic here. The First Witch has come across a woman – a sailor's wife – eating chestnuts. The Witch is recognized and told to go away. But evil cannot be dismissed so easily. The Witch knows about the woman's husband and, with a vindictiveness out of all proportion to her rebuff, she promises to raise a storm and torment the man. The evil is clear; but so too are the all-pervasive nature of the Witches and their association with storms. The master of the *Tiger*, just like Macbeth, will be denied sleep, but because he himself is not wicked (unlike Macbeth) he cannot be destroyed. It is most important to understand that although the forces of evil presented in *Macbeth* are monstrously powerful, they are *not* stronger than the forces of good. The sailor will get home; Malcolm will defeat Macbeth.

A drum announces the arrival of Macbeth and the Witches dance to wind up their magic charms. The spell intensifies the sense of evil just as we first see Macbeth.

We said that *Macbeth* is a play about illusion: things are one thing and seem another – they are ambiguous. The first words that Macbeth speaks are ambiguous: the day is 'foul' because of the storm, 'fair' because of the victory. The good and bad are equally balanced, but from this moment the foul (storm, Witches and evil) are going to predominate both in the play and in Macbeth himself.

The Witches, too, are ambiguous: not natural and yet on earth, they *seem* to understand, they 'should' be women and yet they have beards. Macbeth commands them to speak. They address him very formally, but the repetition of 'All hail, Macbeth!' has a sinister quality about it. How do they know who he is? The titles by which they address him will prove fatal.

You should notice that the Witches *do* nothing to make their prophecies come true and that they always speak the truth. It is humans who make their words come true. Duncan has made Macbeth Thane of Cawdor. Macbeth makes himself king.

He is amazed at what the Witches say, but, significantly, he remains silent. It is Banquo who bursts out and wants to know what is going to happen to him. The immediate excitement of fortune-telling is conveyed by Banquo. The answers he receives are ambiguous: he will not be as great as Macbeth but he will be greater (he won't be king but he will found a line of kings); he won't be so happy but he will be much happier (he won't have a king's power and wealth but he will preserve his integrity), he will be father of a dynasty but he will not be king (Fleance's children will rule Scotland).

Macbeth has been silent all this while. We must imagine what the Witches have said sinking down through the layers of his mind, stirring up the ambition by which he will make their words come true. What they have said to him is all but unbelievable, and he begs to know the source of their power and why they have singled him out in this particular place. The Witches vanish. The source and purpose of evil remain a mystery. Banquo and Macbeth are left amazed.

Ross and Angus enter. Ross reminds us of Macbeth's loyalty and bravery, but now we have seen the Witches the battle seems a long way away. Nonetheless, it is because of the victory that, as Ross now tells him, Macbeth has been made Thane of Cawdor. Amazement! The first of the Witches' prophecies has instantly come true. Their promise of kingship immediately becomes more likely.

Macbeth declares that the Thane of Cawdor is still alive. How can he, Macbeth, have his title? Angus explains that Cawdor is under sentence of death. In his first, brief, crucial aside, Macbeth realizes that the greatest is still to come: kingship. He asks Banquo if he hopes his children will be kings. Banquo is more suspicious; if all the prophecies are indeed fulfilled, then Macbeth will be made king. But how? He declares that evil spirits often tell small truths so that people will believe them and be led into greater danger, even into damnation. He is right, of course; but the thoughtful Macbeth we saw when the Witches first spoke to him now speaks his first major soliloquy. This is important. Much of the development of Macbeth's character in the play is shown through soliloquy. Such speeches obviously show Macbeth on his own, isolated. They also trace the rapid decline of the man of action to a man of words all but paralysed by his conscience. We see this process at work here. The soliloquy records Macbeth's doubt and uses the ambiguous language we have noted before. What the Witches have promised cannot be evil and yet cannot be good. If it is evil, why do they foretell such good news as his being made Thane of Cawdor? However, if it is good, why does it make him think of something so horrible that his hair stands on end and his heart beats faster? In other words, why does it make Macbeth imagine the unimaginable: the murder of his king? He declares at the end of the soliloquy (you should use the notes to make absolutely sure you know what the words mean) that his power to act has been wiped out by his thoughts. Nothing exists for him but his thoughts of the future. As Banquo remarks, Macbeth is obsessed, wrapped in his dreams. The hero and war machine, the great man of action, has become an introvert. As in his later asides, we see Macbeth's realization of the dreadfulness of his obsession. But perhaps, says the man of action who does not want to commit evil, perhaps it will all happen by chance. Time will tell. Macbeth is a changed man. He has to struggle back into the world of Ross, Angus and Banquo who are waiting to take him to the King. He tells Banquo that they must talk about what has happened.

ACT I SCENE iv

Duncan is told that the treacherous Thane of Cawdor has died a good man's death. Yet again, things are ambiguous. People, as Duncan declares, are not always what they seem. And immediately, in comes Macbeth: the man who seems to be a loyal hero but who is already nourishing murder and treason in his heart. Duncan thanks Macbeth for all he has done, telling him that he can never thank him sufficiently. Macbeth replies with an important speech, the wholly correct speech of a loyal subject. Loyalty, he says, is its own reward, and his duty is to his king and country. He is doing what he should when he works for the safety of his king. Seeming to be one thing yet really being another could not be clearer.

Duncan, thinking himself secure, looks to the future. He names Malcolm, his elder son, Prince of Cumberland and his heir. He then declares that he will visit Macbeth in his castle at Dunsinane. This is a further honour. Macbeth says that he will tell his wife of the coming visit, but then plunges immediately into soliloquy. Malcolm has become a threat to him. He is heir to the throne and so is in Macbeth's way. As Macbeth says this, we see his murderous thoughts becoming stronger. He summons up darkness. What he must do must be done invisibly. It is too wicked for daylight. Darkness, evil, the blackening-out of heaven, the murder of the King – all these obsess Macbeth as he leaves the stage. Duncan has no idea of the danger in which he stands.

ACT I SCENE v

Lady Macbeth is reading Macbeth's letter which tells her of his meeting with the Witches and the way in which the first of their prophecies has at once come true. Lady Macbeth knows that he *must* become king, but she knows too that there are weaknesses in Macbeth's character which may prevent this. He has too much compassion to be ruthless. He is 'too full o' the milk of human-kindness', the natural goodness he sucked from his mother. He would like to be great – she knows he is not without ambition – but he lacks the 'illness', the wickedness, necessary. He would like great power, but only wants to get it in an acceptable way. He does not want to be a cheat, but would like to have the rewards of cheating. He would like to be king, and is more afraid of assassinating Duncan than regretful that this should have been done. Again there is ambiguity, illusion, appearance and reality: Macbeth would like to be wicked but, in his wife's opinion, he cannot quite manage to be so.

Just as the Witches greet Macbeth as Thane of Glamis, Thane of Cawdor and future king, so, in imagination, does she. But whereas the Witches merely tell Macbeth what will happen and let the necessary evil ferment in his mind, his wife will actually encourage it. She will chide him into action: actions of evil rather than loyalty. Once more, just as the Witches' first prophecy immediately came true, so Lady Macbeth is immediately given her chance. She is told that Duncan is coming to the castle that night.

Lady Macbeth speaks the second of her great soliloquies. She has already shown herself to be more ambitious than it was thought natural for a woman to be. Now, in this tremendous speech, she tries to expel all natural feelings. In imagination, she summons evil (unnatural) spirits to take away her natural womanly compassion. She wants to be wholly evil, ruthless, empty of natural feelings. Macbeth sucked compassion (which she thinks of as weakness) from his mother's breast. Her breasts must be filled with poison rather than the milk of human kindness. Like her husband, she summons up the night, making more explicit than he the association of night and hell, the idea of evil committed when heaven cannot see.

When Macbeth enters, his wife again greets him as Glamis, Cawdor and future king. He tells her that Duncan is on his way. She asks him when the King is going to leave. His answer, that Duncan plans to leave the next day, shows that Macbeth is far from wanting to murder his king immediately. Lady Macbeth says that the sun will never rise for Duncan again. He will not see tomorrow. They will murder him. Her intention is perfectly clear and she tells Macbeth to seem one thing and be another: to seem the welcoming host yet play the traitor. She tells him to put everything into her hands and, when she has done what she has to do, they will safely be king and queen for the rest of their days. Macbeth wants to discuss the matter further, but she tells him to be resolute and leave everything to her.

The first impression we have of Lady Macbeth is thus one of ambition, power and of a woman who thinks she can be wholly unnatural. Conscience and natural feeling do not worry her in the least. Again, however, Shakespeare is presenting us with reality and illusion. Lady Macbeth seems and wants to make herself a monster of ambition. The discovery of the reality: of conscience, anxiety and natural feeling, the fact that life cannot be led in such a way, will destroy her. We shall see this monster of self-created evil dwindle to the pathetic lunatic of Act V Scene i.

ACT I SCENE vi

Duncan arrives at Macbeth's castle. It *appears* to be a beautiful, healthy and natural place. Birds build their nests there and all seems peaceful and pleasant. Duncan does not know he is walking into hell and to his death.

Lady Macbeth comes out to greet her royal guest. She *appears* to be the perfect hostess, and with a great show of good manners she leads Duncan into the castle and so to his fate.

ACT I SCENE vii

Servants bring on the feast at which Duncan is to be entertained. Macbeth, in sharp contrast, is on his own. The man of action has become a creature of words and doubt, endlessly worried by the consequences of what he wants but cannot bring himself to do.

He would like to get the murder over and done with. He would like to think that to do it would be the end of the business. More sophisticated than his wife, he fears punishment in an afterlife. He fears the effects of his conscience. He is afraid that natural justice will punish him in just proportion to his wickedness. As we do to others, so we shall be done by. Such anguish as Macbeth suffers here is deeply moving. Although he is planning evil, he moves our pity. He is faced with intolerable temptation, but he knows his punishment will be equally intolerable. As he knows and says, there are two very strong reasons why he should not murder Duncan: Duncan is his king (for a discussion of kingship, see pp. 80–82) and his guest. The duty of a host to protect his guests is a sacred one. Macbeth is the very last person to be the murderer. Besides, Duncan is such a good man that pity and the angels will ride storms of indignation so great that the wind will blow the dust of 'the horrid deed' in every eye. The dust and the pity will make every man weep, so much so that the winds will be drowned in tears. Macbeth realizes that it is naked ambition alone which spurs him to action, but it will drive him so hard that he may well be thrown to the ground. The speech is full of doubt and premonition of disaster. The anguish is moving. We feel a once great and loyal man drifting hopelessly towards a course of action he knows not only to be wrong but almost certainly disastrous.

At this point Lady Macbeth enters. Macbeth tries to dissuade her from the murder but she turns on him. Is he a coward? If he is, then she despises his love. Is he frightened of actually doing what he really wants to do? She taunts him mercilessly. The doubts we heard expressed in the soliloquy were those of a fine man. Reinterpreted by Lady Macbeth, they suggest a man who isn't a man at all. Macbeth is made to seem a coward, unworthy of his wife's love. This is an unbearable insult to his pride. Tortured by her, he turns and says (reminding us he is indeed a hero) that he can do anything a man can do. Who wants to go further than that is not a man but an unnatural monster.

No, says Lady Macbeth, Macbeth was a real man when he first suggested the idea of murder to her. (Did he? Wasn't it she who developed the plan?) When he wanted to make himself king, she says, then he was indeed a man. When there was no opportunity of murdering Duncan, he wished an opportunity existed. Now the chance has fallen into their lap. With what result? He is terrified, a coward. In lines that make her dreadful unnaturalness abundantly clear, Lady Macbeth says she would dash the brains out of her own children if they got in the way of an opportunity like this.

But what if we should fail? Macbeth asks.

Lady Macbeth is contemptuous of such an idea and rapidly she outlines the details of her plan, describing it in such a way that Macbeth's courage will be roused and his fears put aside. When Duncan is asleep she will make his grooms drunk, and then she and her husband will be able to do whatever they like to him. People will blame the grooms and say that they committed the murder in a drunken fury. It is a safe, deeply cowardly plan, and it wins the hero over. Macbeth is delighted. His wife has solved his problems. He can seize the throne and seize it safely. No one will accuse him. He has what he wants now. He has won back his courage (courage to kill a sleeping man) and he has won back his wife's love. The first Act ends with a newly resolved Macbeth, a man confident that he can kill his king and confident that he can *seem* the host while relishing the idea of being a murderer.

ACT II SCENE i

It is a little after midnight and Banquo is going to bed. His son helps him disarm. Banquo longs for sleep but is troubled by his thoughts. The atmosphere of suspicion grows as he hears a noise and demands his sword again. The threat is none other than Macbeth wandering through the castle. Banquo comments that the King has been generous and has enjoyed himself at the feast. He mentions the Witches. Macbeth, lying to the man who was once a close friend, says he doesn't think about them but will willingly talk about them at some other time. Macbeth tells Banquo that if he allies with him, then, should he become king, Banquo will do well. Macbeth is trying to buy him. Banquo says he will go along with Macbeth provided he is not compromised. This may well make us wonder if Banquo is already suspicious of Macbeth.

They part. Macbeth sends a servant to tell his wife to ring a bell when his drink is ready. The bell is, of course, the cue for the murder.

Again Macbeth is alone, this time in the silence and darkness of the midnight castle. He has sworn to murder Duncan and his doubts are quietened in his new resolve. His mind is not easy, however. In his desperately nervous state he imagines a dagger floating before him, the dagger with which he will murder Duncan. He reaches out for it, wondering if it is real or a hallucination. It continues to float before him. It seems to be leading him to the King's presence. Blood appears on it. Macbeth tries to dismiss it, realizing that he is overwrought. He becomes aware of the dark, silent world around him. Nature and natural feeling seem dead. It is a time of false and wicked dreams, of witchcraft, murder, wolves and rape. As Macbeth talks of these things, they seem to become a part of him, to make his evil really clear. The suspicion and suspense mount as Macbeth begs the earth not to hear his footsteps, for the sound on the flagstones may give him away. Silence best suits what he is to do, but such talk as this cools the ardour of action. The bell rings. The moment has come. It is a knell (a bell rung at a funeral) which summons Duncan to heaven or hell.

ACT II SCENE ii

Lady Macbeth enters. Her pretence of heroic evil is already beginning to give way. She has been drinking, but for all her bravado, she jumps at the shriek of an owl. 'He is about it,' she says: a grim, terse description of the murder of the King. Macbeth calls out in the darkness. For a second she is frightened that he may have been caught. She has put the daggers out in readiness, she says, and he could not have missed them. Then we have the first major revelation: when she saw Duncan sleeping he reminded her of her father. Her pity was stronger than her cruelty and she could not kill him. She, who was so ready to ignore conscience and commit the murder herself, found that she was unable to do so. For all her brave, terrible words and her accusation of Macbeth's cowardice, she could not do the deed. Macbeth proves himself the man of action. Here is tragic irony.

He comes in with the bloodstained daggers. She greets him and he declares that he has 'done the deed'. He, too, is jumpy, and the quick exchange of question and answer seems to highlight this. Then, looking down at his bloody hands, remorse sweeps over Macbeth – 'This is a sorry sight.' Lady Macbeth tells him he is being foolish. Again she believes she can banish conscience by an effort of will, but the depth of Macbeth's guilt and the realization that he has cut himself off from both God and future rest become movingly clear.

As he was going to the King's chamber he heard a sleeping couple: one laughed in his sleep, the other cried 'Murder!' They woke each other. Macbeth heard them, heard them say their prayers and then turn over and try to get to sleep again. Lady Macbeth explains that two of the guests have been given the same room. But for Macbeth the horror is more than noises in the dark. As the two prayed he heard one cry 'God bless us' and the other reply 'Amen', as though they had spoken in fear of him. These men have an easy access to God. *They* can pray. Macbeth cannot. The word 'Amen' sticks in his throat and he knows he is cut off from God, from goodness and the natural order of the world.

Lady Macbeth, still believing that willpower can conquer all, tells him not to think like this or he will go mad. It is she, of course, riddled with the guilt she cannot suppress, who will indeed end up insane. Macbeth goes on to say that he heard another voice which told him that he would never sleep again. Just as he has lost contact with God by slaying the Lord's anointed king (see 'The Nature of Kingship', pp. 80–82), so he has lost all chance of sleep, of the rest offered by the natural world. Cut off from God and sleep, he will suffer an anguish of restlessness in a godless world without sense or order.

He has guessed at the truth, seen how his life will be. His wife tells him to pull himself together. What are these voices? she asks. As always, she tries to offset Macbeth's anguish by being strictly practical. She tells him to go and wash the blood off his hands. Seeing the daggers, she realizes that they must be put beside the grooms if these men are to be blamed for the deed. She orders Macbeth to take them back. He cannot return to the room. Lady Macbeth, contemptuous of him, tells him that dead bodies are no more frightening than sleeping ones. Taking the daggers, she declares that if the King is still bleeding she will smear the grooms with his blood.

Macbeth is alone again, but, rather than have him plunge into doubt, Shakespeare has other purposes. The worst possible of all crimes against the state has taken place: the King has been murdered. The ruler of the state, appointed by God, is dead. At this point, where evil has apparently triumphed, Shakespeare has to show that good does exist in the world, that evil does not go undetected. Through the murderer's castle, at midnight, the knocking of Macduff and Lennox at the gate is heard. For the moment we do not know it is them. All we hear is the noise that terrifies Macbeth. He looks down at his bloody hands and becomes aware that he will never be able to wash the gore from them. For the rest of his life he will be polluted with his master's blood.

Lady Macbeth re-enters and chides him for his cowardice. She, too, hears the knocking and she realizes that they must seem to have been in bed. 'A little water,' she says, 'clears us of this deed.' She does not understand as Macbeth does (and this is what gives him his tragic stature) that she will never be free from guilt. She does not have his moral awareness. For the moment she does not suffer as he does. She lives in the practical world. When she hears the knocking again, she knows they must get into their nightclothes so that it will seem that they have been in bed all the time. But Macbeth is convinced that he is lost. It is nothing to get away with the murder in the sight of the world. By murdering his king he has cut himself off for ever from God, peace and contentment.

ACT II SCENE iii

The 'Porter scene' is a deliberately comic contrast. For the moment we have had all we can take of horror. Besides, when Macduff and Lennox finally gain admission to the castle, the murder moves on to a new, public level. We shall see how it affects not only Macbeth and his wife, but the whole of Scotland.

The Porter is drunk and talkative. As he shambles towards the gate of Macbeth's castle, he sees it in his imagination as the gate of hell. This is both amusing and a comment on what has happened. With Duncan lying dead in his chamber and Macbeth and his wife committed to the forces of evil, the castle is indeed hell on earth.

As he stumbles to the door, the Porter imagines three new arrivals in hell: a farmer who, storing his crops and hoping prices would rise, was disappointed and so hanged himself. Suicide is the traditional expression of despair and we should recall that it is suspected at the very end of the play that the despairing Lady Macbeth has taken her own life. The second of the imaginary callers is an 'equivocator' (a man who swears to the truth of one thing while believing another). Equivocation, of course, is central to *Macbeth*: the Witches' prophecies are interpreted one way but in fact mean something else; Macbeth appears as a loyal hero but is in fact a traitor; Lady Macbeth appears a tower of evil strength but dwindles to a pathetic wreck. The third imagined guest is a thief, a tailor who has sold his customers short. Despair, two-facedness and theft: all these lead to hell; all of them characterize Macbeth and his wife.

But evil is not all-powerful. The entry of Macduff is the first faint beginning of hope. We have barely seen him so far. We shall now watch him grow through suffering and moral strength to be the man who finally kills Macbeth.

Macduff is not without a sense of humour and leads the Porter on to muse on drink, the provoker of three things: a red nose, sleep and urine. As far as a man's sexuality is concerned, drink is an equivocator: it heightens his interest but stops him having an erection. Macduff replies with a good-hearted pun: drink, he says, gave the Porter 'the lie' last night, in other words, it spoiled his sexual performance, made him urinate, and tripped him up. The Porter makes an equally witty reply. Building on the idea of being tripped up, he pretends he has been wrestling with drink who did manage to topple him over sometimes, although the Porter tried to 'cast' him – meaning both to throw him down and to sick up.

This gross physical joking has an important purpose: laughter cleans us out. When Macduff finally enters the castle we are fresh for new horror.

Macduff immediately encounters Macbeth who, equivocating, tries to give the impression that nothing out of the ordinary has happened. Macduff has called early for the King, but Duncan is not awake and Macbeth offers to bring Macduff to him.

The first indication that something is very wrong comes from Lennox. He tells of the terrible storm that broke the previous night and the awful supernatural noises that were heard. Chimneys were blown down and owls hooted all night long. This is a description of evil and chaos in nature, evil and chaos that have been unleashed by Macbeth's murder of Duncan. Without its God-appointed king, the whole state is threatened with destruction. Macbeth agrees tersely with Lennox. It was 'a rough night'.

Crying out, Macduff re-enters. He has seen the unimaginable and the indescribable: the murdered body of Duncan. In words that explain the significance of the murder of kings, he declares that confusion has 'made his masterpiece'. Duncan, whose body is compared to the holy temple, has been murdered. This is a sacrilege, a crime against God. Macduff says the sight is so terrible that it will turn all onlookers to stone. Macbeth (keeping up appearances) and Lennox rush off to investigate. Macduff orders the alarm bell to be rung and wakes Banquo and Donalbain. We must imagine an enormous outburst of noise here as the public repercussions of the murder come to the fore after the silence of the midnight castle when the murder took place.

The noise is certainly enough to bring Lady Macbeth to the scene. She asks what is the matter. She gives a convincing impression of ignorance, and is told that what has happened is so dreadful that a woman should not hear about it. Macduff tells Banquo, who has also been roused by the noise.

Macbeth re-enters and what he has to say is of the greatest significance. It is a public speech, a speech designed to show his despair, as a loyal subject, at Duncan's murder. He declares that if he had died an hour before then he would have lived a good life in a holy time, a time when all was well because a God-appointed king preserved the true order and security of the world. Now, with the death of the King, there is no more order, holiness or security. 'Renown and grace', the best things in life, are dead. All is meaningless and bitter. It is the truth of this that Macbeth has to discover in the rest of the play: the horrible truth of a life without God, without order and with no more purpose than the hopeless and increasingly bloody business of trying to keep himself secure. The greatness of Macbeth lies in his experience of this, in his deeply poetic expression of the futility of his life. From this moment on he becomes ever more tyrannical and bloody, ever more cruel, a monster and a tyrant; but – and this is the crucial point – he is not simply a man becoming even lower than the beasts. He is the wreck of a great man who suffers and understands the consequences of what he has done. He is both unforgivable yet profoundly moving.

All this will come later. For the moment, everything is hectic activity. Malcolm and Donalbain have been roused by the clamour and are told that their father has been killed. They ask who is the murderer, and Lady Macbeth's alibi seems to hold. Lennox declares that Duncan was murdered by the drunken grooms.

Macbeth begins to construct a world of lies in which he is increasingly enmeshed. He declares that he killed the grooms because the sight of the murdered Duncan drove him wild. He has, of course, murdered them so that they will never wake to tell the truth or protest their innocence. This double murder is the first of many that Macbeth will have to commit in the desperate and hopeless attempt to make himself secure.

Lady Macbeth faints and Banquo orders her to be carried out, suggesting that they all meet later to discuss the consequences of the murder. Banquo puts himself in God's hands in the investigation of this treason. By doing so he can only make himself an enemy of Macbeth who agrees that they must indeed meet to discuss what has happened.

Left on their own, the King's two sons, Malcolm and Donalbain, agree on flight. They realize immediately that they stand in great danger: suspicion will obviously fall on them as they apparently stand to gain most by Duncan's murder. Malcolm declares that he will go to England, while Donalbain elects to go to Ireland. They are safer apart. There are, as Donalbain says, 'daggers in men's smiles'. It is a brilliant image of the danger and two-facedness that will now prevail in Scotland. Malcolm, who has not been thoroughly developed as a character yet, says that flight is indeed the wisest political move and quite legitimate in the circumstances. Our first real understanding of Malcolm is as an astute young man as well as the rightful king. In this may lie some hope.

ACT II SCENE iv

This short scene between Ross (who is a relatively unimportant character) and the Old Man who is not even named is significant for the way in which it shows the effects of the murder of the King on the people of Scotland as a whole. The Old Man can remember many terrible things but nothing as bad as the storm that broke last night. Heaven, as Ross declares, is troubled by the murder. Divine justice is not indifferent. The murder (and, by implication, Macbeth) have brought enduring darkness to Scotland. As the Old Man says, it is 'unnatural'. By the murder of Duncan the order of nature has been destroyed, and with it peace and harmony. Even the animals behave in strange and unnatural ways. Macduff, entering, confirms that current opinion has it that the murder was committed by the grooms, bribed by Malcolm and Donalbain, whose flight only makes their guilt look yet more certain. This also seems unnatural. Ross supposes that Macbeth will be the next king (this is in fact his right by birth now that Duncan and his sons are out of the way). Macduff confirms that Macbeth has already gone to be crowned in Scone, where Ross now goes. Macduff, significantly, does not attend the coronation but goes quickly to his home in Fife.

ACT III SCENE i

Banquo certainly has his suspicions. His soliloquy at the beginning of the third act shows that he realizes how the prophecies of the Witches have been fulfilled. Macbeth is 'King, Cawdor, Glamis, all/As the weird women promised'. He is virtually certain Macbeth has murdered to achieve this. Banquo thinks of what was promised him: that he would be the founder of a dynasty. What the Witches say seems to come true. Why, then, should he not hope? Clearly he has forgotten the details of what they said: 'Thou shalt get kings, though thou be none.' He will not be king, of course, because Macbeth will have to murder him to get him out of the way. Banquo is a danger of which Macbeth is fully aware. He and his wife flatter him when they meet him. As king and queen they are the source of wealth and power, but it becomes clear that Macbeth has made his plans. He questions Banquo closely about an afternoon ride he proposes to take and, to cover suspicion, repeats the invitation to a great feast that night. He is careful also to remind Banquo that it was Malcolm and Donalbain who killed Duncan. Remembering it was prophesied that Banquo would be father to a line of kings, Macbeth finds out if Banquo's son Fleance is riding with his father. He learns that he is. Macbeth then declares that he is going to withdraw until the time of the banquet. As the court and Lady Macbeth exit he calls his servant and asks if 'those men' are waiting for him. They, of course, are to be the murderers of Banquo.

Alone, Macbeth soliloquizes. He knows he is not safe. Banquo and his noble nature are dangerous. He feels that somehow Banquo has power over him. His mind does not function properly in his presence. Besides, the Witches 'hailed him father to a line of kings'. This is the greatest threat. If Banquo's children do indeed succeed to the throne (which, of course, they will) then Macbeth's kingship is a mockery. He has destroyed his peace of mind and sold his soul to the devil for nothing; for nothing, he bitterly reflects, but to make Banquo's children kings, thereby fulfilling the Witches' prophecies.

We see here a man alone in his evil and aware of its seriousness. We see also the restless, endless doubt and suspicion Macbeth is locked in. We see thirdly (and perhaps most cruelly) the fact that he believes the

Witches' prophecies can be altered or made to fit his own good. If he can kill Banquo and Fleance then he is safe. But the Witches' prophecies always come true; Macbeth is *not* the master of his fate. He will try to have Banquo and Fleance removed, but Fleance will escape and found, through his children, a new dynasty of kings. Macbeth cannot invalidate the Witches' prophecies. He can only work to make them come true.

Nonetheless, he believes for the moment that he is master of his destiny. He summons the two Murderers whom he hopes will make him safe. He has already met them once before (this brilliantly gives the impression that even we in the audience do not know everything that is going on in Macbeth's mind, that we have not been told all his plans) and he now reminds them that on the previous occasion he made them believe it was Banquo who had been responsible for the wrongs they had suffered. You should note that only at the end of the speech is it made clear that Macbeth is piling the suspicion on Banquo. Macbeth now tries to rouse the men's fury against Banquo rather in the way that Lady Macbeth tried to rouse his own ambition. The Murderers are low, wretched, desperate men. Macbeth asks them if they are cowards. Are they so 'good' that they will not seek revenge? 'We are men, my liege,' the First Murderer pitifully replies. Macbeth pretends to be less sure. Taking dogs as his example, he says that there are many different types of dog, with many different qualities. It is these distinctions that are important. If the Murderers are indeed men and 'not i' the worst rank of manhood' (in other words, not cowards) Macbeth will give them the means whereby they can dispose of their enemy Banquo and earn the love of their new king, who, for his part, feels threatened by Banquo and knows he will be safe if he is rid of him.

The Murderers confess that they have been brought so low and are so desperate that they don't care what they do.

Macbeth is well pleased. He presents Banquo as his most dangerous enemy (which, of course, though not for the reasons of state Macbeth hints at, he is). But, he declares, he does not want to seem to be a tyrant and publicly obliterate Banquo. He and Banquo have common friends who would be dangerously upset by such a procedure. The murder has to be committed in secret. The atmosphere of suspicion that characterizes Macbeth's rule deepens.

The Murderers say they will do as they are asked. Macbeth tells them he will outline the details of his plan later. By saying the murder must be committed 'tonight' the suggestion of nervousness, even the continuous panic which is now Macbeth's state, is made clear. He adds that Fleance must also 'embrace the fate/Of that dark hour'. The Murderers declare themselves 'resolved' and, left alone, Macbeth is triumphant in what he is sure will be his safety.

ACT III SCENE ii

Lady Macbeth asks her servant if Banquo has gone. On being told that he has, she sends the servant to her husband to tell him she wants to talk with him.

Left alone, it is clear that she, too, is suffering from the same restless doubt, the endless suspicion to which the crime has exposed her. Where, we should ask, is the woman of heroically evil resolve, the woman who believed that 'a little water clears us of this deed'? She cannot live free from conscience. She is discovering what Macbeth already knows: conscience returns to plague the authors of evil. It would be better to be dead, she declares, than to live as she does now, 'in doubtful joy'.

But her own doubts must be hidden. She is well aware of the pains of conscience Macbeth is suffering and she knows that she must constantly chide him, brace him for whatever he must do to keep them safe. Despite her own despair, she tells her husband not to think in this way. There is nothing they can do: 'What's done is done.'

Macbeth reminds her of the dangers that remain. Danger (personified in Banquo) is still a poisonous snake. They wounded it (when they killed the grooms); they have not destroyed it. But it would be better that heaven and earth should perish rather than that they should always eat their meals in fear and wake each night from bad dreams. To be dead would be better, to be dead as Duncan is now would be better 'Than on the torture of the mind to lie/In restless ecstasy'. The images of the restlessness that will wear them both down and finally break Lady Macbeth are most powerful here. They are made the more so by Macbeth's bitterly ironic envy of Duncan's sleep of death: '... nothing/Can touch him further'.

With somewhat desperate affection, Lady Macbeth bids her husband be cheerful (and so two-faced) at the banquet that evening. Her tenderness here seems to come partly from her own desperation, her need for love and security. She cannot live lovelessly with her guilt. That she should play the comforting wife at this point is pathetically ironic, but we should note that as her power dwindles, so Macbeth seems to take over the initiative. Just before the murder the man of action was all but paralysed by doubt. His wife was the chief driving force. Now he can advise her to put on a happy face at the feast. In so doing he is sickened by his hypocrisy. Again his wife chides him, and he breaks out with the most vivid image of suffering: scorpions crawling on his brain. She knows, he says, that Banquo and Fleance are still alive. She replies that indeed she does, but they will not, cannot, live for ever. He agrees with her: 'They are assailable'. He summons up images of evil magic to surround his hint of a 'deed of dreadful note'. Lady Macbeth asks him what he means, but he will not tell her his plan. With an ironic tenderness, he bids her be 'innocent of the knowledge'. Macbeth has now clearly taken the initiative in evil from his wife, and we feel the growing independence and desperate strength of his wickedness. By the most bitter of ironies, the once all but immobilized man of action recovers his abilities as he is led ever further into wickedness. His speech concludes with a magnificent identification of night and evil. Night will hide the sun and destroy the laws of nature and humanity. As light fails, the crow flies to the wood. Evil creatures of the night rouse themselves, Macbeth amongst them. Summoning up evil in this way, Macbeth seems also to summon up his own resolve. Both the audience and Lady Macbeth marvel at him. Tragically, he believes that evil can be secured by more evil. The only (and hopeless) hope in Macbeth's perverted world is that two wrongs can somehow make a right.

ACT III SCENE iii

After so much suspicious talk we need action. We are shown the murder of Banquo and the attempt on Fleance.

The two Murderers are joined by a third and the atmosphere of mistrust deepens. The three men hear Banquo and Fleance galloping towards them in the dark, and when they are close enough to strike they do so by the light of Banquo's own lamp. The dying Banquo bids Fleance fly. The boy is safe. He escapes to fulfil his own fate and the Witches' prophecy. The Murderers, left in the darkness, realize they have only killed Banquo and have bungled their task.

ACT III SCENE iv

We move from a scene of wild and desolate murder to the mirth and apparent safety of a feast. Macbeth, true to his word, welcomes his guests and plays the good host by moving among them. He even goes so far as to chide Lady Macbeth lightly for not joining in. She bids Macbeth say for her how welcome they all are. As Macbeth shows her how happy the guests seem and, with great friendliness, sits among them, the First Murderer enters. We should imagine Macbeth, in a moment of great sociability, suddenly turning cold. He sees blood on the Murderer's face. He praises the man when he is told the blood is Banquo's, but when he is informed that 'Fleance is scaped', panic and insecurity come to him again. With Fleance dead he would have been safe, strong and free. Now fear will make his life a claustrophobic hell. He tells the Murderer to return the next day.

This desperate private conversation is at odds with the conviviality of the feast, as Lady Macbeth reminds her husband. To make up for it, Macbeth proposes a toast.

The bloody-faced Murderer first reminded us of the cold horror from which Macbeth can never escape. The entrance later of Banquo's ghost (invisible to all but Macbeth) makes this vividly clear. Ironically, it is the absence of Banquo that Macbeth first chooses to talk about, comforting himself and boasting about what he supposes to be his own safety. Lennox bids him sit down, and, as he does so, Macbeth sees the murdered Banquo's ghost. He turns on the guests: 'Which of you have done this?' The guests are surprised because they cannot see anything, cannot see what has caused Macbeth's sudden, hysterical chill. Macbeth cannot accept responsibility for the murder. 'Thou canst not say I did it,' Macbeth tells the ghost of Banquo. 'Never shake/Thy gory locks at me.' Morally, of course, Macbeth *is* responsible for the murder.

Ross tries to cover the acute embarrassment of the guests (who cannot see the ghost) by saying that Macbeth is ill and that they should leave him. Lady Macbeth, summoning all her powers, bids them sit down and tries to excuse her husband's behaviour by inventing the idea that he has suffered from an illness since his youth. The fit is nothing and will soon be over. They should not take any notice of him, for attention makes him worse. Lady Macbeth, like the others, cannot see the ghost and thus cannot understand the reason for Macbeth's hysteria. She rounds on him and says that his behaviour is as weak and hysterical now as when he believed he saw the dagger. Both visions are ridiculous, like ghost stories told by old women. He ought to be ashamed of himself. There is nothing for him to see except a stool – the stool left empty for Banquo. The ghost is vivid enough to Macbeth, however. His speech breaks down. There is no point, he says, in burying the dead if they rise from their graves. We should just leave their bodies for birds of prey. The ghost disappears, but Macbeth is thoroughly shaken.

Lady Macbeth desperately reminds him of his duties as host, and for a few brave seconds Macbeth pulls himself together and tries to excuse himself on the grounds of the illness his wife has mentioned. He proposes another toast, this time to Banquo. This is replied to, and again the ghost appears. Macbeth shouts at it to go, to hide in the earth. Banquo's body is cold, the glaring eyes of the ghost in fact are sightless. Macbeth says, truly, that he is as brave as any man alive. He would face the wildest beast without fear – face anything, indeed, except a ghost. If Banquo were to come back alive he would challenge him to single combat. He shouts at the ghost to disappear and, as a dreadful anticlimax, it does so.

With its disappearance, Macbeth can say he is 'a man again'. But it is no good. He has ruined the feast. For his part he is amazed that others can look on the ghost with no apparent reaction. He does not understand that the ghost haunts only him, that it is his special torture. He wonders that his guests can 'behold such sights/And keep the natural ruby of your cheeks,/When mine is blanched with fear'. Ross asks him what he means, but Lady Macbeth, realizing that further questions might be dangerous, orders the guests to leave as quickly as possible. They do so.

Macbeth is left muttering that murder will out, the mysteries of nature will betray it. Pathetic, exhausted, he turns to his wife and asks her the time. It is almost, but not quite, dawn. Even the time is equivocal.

Remembering his endless insecurities, Macbeth wonders why Macduff (who was absent from his coronation) failed to come to the feast. He must find out. A true tyrant running a tyrant's state, he keeps double agents in all the nobles' houses. But such systems are not enough. Macbeth feels he must have real assurance. Tomorrow he will go early to the Witches. He *will* find out more. Pathetically, he believes that they can put his mind at rest. He does not care what the cost may be. As he says, he has now shed so much blood, rivers of it, that should he shed no more, wading back would be just as hard work as crossing over to the other side. But Macbeth cannot go back. He will have to go on shedding blood. The plans he has are such that he will have to act quickly. He has no more time for careful plotting. Lady Macbeth begs him to sleep. He admits that his strange behaviour on seeing Banquo's ghost was due to his inexperience in crime.

ACT III SCENE v

We meet the Witches again. Just as there is chaos in Scotland, so there is in their kingdom. Their ruler, Hecate, is furious that they have presumed to deal with Macbeth without her. And, she adds, they have done this not for a man who wants to glorify them but for one who seeks to glorify himself. The Witches must make amends by meeting Hecate the following morning by a river of hell (Acheron), where she knows Macbeth will come to learn his fate. They must be fully prepared for her since, by catching a drop hanging on the tip of the moon, they will raise 'such artificial sprites' that Macbeth will be drawn to madness. They will show him things so terrible that he will become reckless. By removing reasonable fear from Macbeth in this way they will ensure his damnation. The Witches dance and sing until Hecate, called by her familiar spirit, leaves. The others also depart.

ACT III SCENE vi

Just as Act II Scene iv showed the effects of Duncan's murder on Scotland, Scene vi shows the effects of Macbeth's tyranny on the people of Scotland. This is a difficult scene. Lennox's language in particular is hard to interpret. There is a reason for this: Shakespeare wanted to show that people living under tyranny cannot speak straightforwardly. They are too frightened to do so. They have to work by hints and suggestions. Lennox and the nameless Lord recognize that they are in agreement. Both know that things in Scotland are not as they should be: Macbeth pitied Duncan *when he was dead*; Banquo *was* out late, a dangerous thing to be; you can say *if you like* that Fleance killed him. Certainly Fleance fled. Certainly it was dreadful of Malcolm and Donalbain to kill their father. Macbeth was certainly so upset by it that he murdered the grooms. That was noble. After all, anybody would have been made angry by hearing them protest their innocence. The implication, of course, is that Macbeth is behind all this and that he has covered his traces well, but not quite well enough. No doubt if he caught Malcolm, Donalbain and Fleance they would rapidly be sentenced to death for murdering their fathers. That, after all, would get them out of the way. But Lennox realizes that even this convoluted speech could be dangerous and turns to comment on Macduff, who is living in disgrace.

The unnamed Lord replies that Malcolm is in England at the court of 'the most pious Edward'. He is being joined there by Macduff, whose plan is to ask Edward to raise forces to invade Scotland and return normal, everyday peace to the country. It is hoped God will help in this. Peace is desperately needed. He concludes by saying that Macbeth knows about Macduff's reception in England and is preparing for war. The Lord asks if Macduff is involved in Macbeth's preparations. It seems Macduff has refused to help Macbeth, a fact which has annoyed Macbeth's messenger, who may well forfeit advancement if he brings bad news. Lennox declares that Macduff should be very careful. He wishes that an angel would fly to England with supernatural speed and so deliver Macduff's message before Macduff himself can arrive. The state of Scotland is desperate.

ACT IV SCENE i

The appearance of the Witches is again announced by thunder, symbolizing the forces of chaos they unleash. The repetitious chanting of their words and the vividly realized details of what they throw into their cauldron give a strong impression of evil. The Witches have gathered the most revolting reptiles, the most venomous snakes, even the finger of a murdered bastard baby. The effect is at once sordid and threatening.

Hecate enters when their charm is ready. She bids them dance around the cauldron as they wait for Macbeth's arrival and the chance to fulfil Hecate's wish to drive him mad. The Second Witch's thumbs prick as she feels something wicked approaching. It is Macbeth. He rudely asks the Witches what they are doing and all three reply: 'A deed without a name.' The casting of the spell, the preparation of their magic, is evil beyond the power of words to describe.

The Witches know, of course, that Macbeth is going to come and they know why. They are prepared for him. He does not understand this and forcefully, wordily, cries out that they should answer his questions. The simplicity of their answers is a crushing anticlimax to the excited Macbeth who is asked whether he would prefer to hear the truth from them or their masters. He tersely asks them to summon their masters. They pour the blood of a sow who has eaten her young and the sweat of a hanged man into their cauldron. The First Apparition, in the form of an armed head, appears. Macbeth tries to order it to speak. He still believes that he has some sort of authority. The Witches tell him the Apparition can read his mind. He is not to talk to it. He must simply listen. The First Apparition tells Macbeth to beware of Macduff. Macbeth is comforted by this supernatural support of his own suspicions. The Apparition disappears.

The Second Apparition, in the form of a bloody child, calls to Macbeth and tells him he can laugh the power of men to scorn: 'for none of woman born/Shall harm Macbeth'. This seems to provide Macbeth with total security, but, though he realizes that this apparently means he has nothing to fear from Macduff, he will 'make assurance double sure' and murder him. Macbeth's desperate ruthlessness is gaining ground.

The Third Apparition, 'a Child crowned, with a tree in his hand', appears. Macbeth asks what it represents but is again told to listen but not speak. The child tells Macbeth he has nothing to fear 'until/Great Birnan Wood to high Dunsinane Hill/Shall come against him'. Macbeth thinks it impossible that the trees could ever march against his castle. He derives great joy from his entirely misplaced sense of security. But he wants to know one more thing: will Banquo's children rule in Scotland? Will this prophecy come true? The Witches advise him to 'seek to know no more'. Macbeth breaks out furiously. He *must* know. Not realizing that they are the damned, he says he wishes them cursed if they will not tell him. Mysteriously the cauldron sinks, music is heard and the Witches present the last and, for Macbeth, the cruellest of their apparitions. Eight kings move wordlessly across the stage accompanied by Banquo. Macbeth watches with increasing horror. He feels his eyeballs burn. He curses the Witches. The procession seems to stretch on for ever ... seven, eight, and the last king holds a glass in which many future generations (up to and beyond Shakespeare's patron James I) appear. Banquo smiles at Macbeth and shows that the kings are indeed his descendants. Macbeth asks desperately if this is the case.

It is. The murder of Duncan has given Macbeth nothing. He has destroyed himself, his peace, his soul, and achieved no permanent success. He will not found a line of kings. The Witches' prophecies *will* come true. Banquo's children *will* become kings. The Witches, in a grossly ironic gesture, dance for Macbeth and disappear. He is left alone, cursing the hour.

Lennox appears. Has he seen the Witches? No. They have appeared only for Macbeth, for his particular damnation. They have ridden silently away into the air. Only the sound of earthly horses is heard. Macbeth is told that they are messengers come to inform him of Macduff's flight to England. Macbeth's reaction here is of the greatest importance.

Hecate has promised that she will drive Macbeth mad. He will lose all self-control, all sense of proportion and of right and wrong. We now see this happen. Macduff has fled. This is deeply suspicious, but rather than think out the consequences, Macbeth declares that he will do the first thing that comes into his head:

> *From this moment*
> *The very firstlings of my heart shall be*
> *The firstlings of my hand.*

He will surprise Macduff's castle, seize Fife and slaughter Lady Macduff, his children and all his relations. He will do it now. He will rush blindly into action before thoughts cool his purpose. There is no longer any trace in Macbeth of the rational man of action. He doesn't want to think any more. He has abandoned reason and has become a homicidal maniac, a mass exterminator in the manner of tyrants like Hitler and Stalin.

ACT IV SCENE ii

The scene opens with the first victims of Macbeth's total lunacy: Lady Macduff and her son.

Lady Macduff is talking with Ross. She is angry and upset that her husband has fled to England and left her unprotected. She knows how savage nature can be and thinks only in terms of her own imminent death. Ross tries to comfort her. The times are cruel and uncertain with a tyrant on the throne. Ross leaves her but promises to return.

Left with her son, Lady Macduff talks to him. She believes that his father is dead. How will the little boy live now? Like a bird, he replies, getting what he can. The child does not believe his father is dead, but his mother insists that he is. He asks her what she will do for a husband? She deflects the seriousness of his question by saying that she can buy twenty at any market. The boy asks if his father was a traitor, and then asks what a traitor is. A traitor, he is told, is 'one that swears and lies'. He must be hanged. The little boy cannot understand this. He knows there are more liars and swearers than honest men, so it is the honest men who should look out. The little boy babbles on. This is a scene of great tenderness and simplicity: deliberately so. It is precisely such charming innocence Macbeth will destroy. A Messenger warns them both to fly. The distraught Lady Macduff asks where they can go. There is no escape. The horrific, anonymous Murderers enter, ask for Macduff, and call him a traitor. The boy tells them they are lying and is stabbed. Dying, he bids his mother fly. She is chased through the castle and is eventually murdered.

ACT IV SCENE iii

This is the longest scene in the play and takes place in England. Macduff has arrived and he and Malcolm are describing the state of Scotland. Up to this point, the character of Malcolm has barely been developed. We know that he has been named the legitimate heir (I, iv, ll. 35–42) and we have seen that he is fairly worldly-wise (II, iii). Now both these aspects are more clearly defined.

Malcolm allows himself to be encouraged by Macduff, but the tale he has to tell him is one of continuous sorrow in Scotland. Malcolm shows that he is moved but, as he points out, it may well be to Macduff's advantage to sell the young and innocent Malcolm to Macbeth. In other words, is Macduff a double agent? Macduff roundly declares that he is not a traitor. But, as Malcolm tells him, Macbeth is, and he may be a sufficiently powerful figure to tempt Macduff to his side. It is clear to Malcolm, however, that Macduff is a man of integrity. Malcolm cannot even in imagination make him a traitor. Goodness does indeed shine through. He then asks Macduff why he has left his wife and children in Scotland without even saying goodbye to them. Are they to be safe if, and only if, Macduff betrays Malcolm to Macbeth? We see that young Malcolm is very circumspect indeed. Macduff is so disappointed by this depth of suspicion on Malcolm's part that he decides that the best thing for him is to leave. Clearly Malcolm is too full of doubts to act for the good and, as a result, Macbeth is safe. Scotland will continue to bleed under his tyranny.

Malcolm begs Macduff not to be offended. He is testing him. He is not really suspicious of him. He is just making absolutely sure of him. He knows how much Scotland is suffering and he is grateful for support from England; but when he gets the crown back, he says, rightful king though he is, things will be far worse for Scotland than ever they were before. He himself is so full of vices that the future of his country will be grim indeed.

This, of course, is not true. Malcolm has cleared Macduff of all suspicion of being a double agent. He now wants to test him to see whether his loyalty to the rightful heir to the throne is strong, whatever weaknesses Malcolm may have or pretend to have.

Macduff asks Malcolm to explain himself and is told that he, Malcolm, is far more wicked than Macbeth. The range of his vices will make 'black Macbeth' look as 'pure as snow'. Macduff says this is impossible. There is no devil in hell worse than Macbeth. Malcolm says Macbeth is indeed bloody, luxury-loving, avaricious, a liar and a man prone to act impetuously. But he, Malcolm, is sensuous beyond belief. If he slept with every woman in the country his lust would not be sated, and his desire admits no obstacle. Macduff admits that this is a serious fault ('Boundless intemperance/In nature is a tyranny'), but there are enough women in Scotland – indeed more than enough – who would be willing to offer themselves to a prince.

But this is not all. Malcolm also declares himself to be an avaricious man with an insatiable desire for money. He will steal and trick wealth out of all his subjects. Macduff sees this as a more serious fault than 'summer-seeming lust'. But, he says, reluctantly, Scotland is rich enough to cope with this.

Malcolm finally declares that he has none of the 'king-becoming graces', he hates such virtues and loves crime. He would willingly plunge the world into chaos.

At this point, Macduff realizes that there is no hope. He openly grieves for Scotland. Malcolm asks if such a man is fit to govern Scotland. No, replies Macduff, not fit even to live. Poor Scotland, ruled by a tyrant while the legitimate heir is a man like this! When will she know peace again? Macduff points out that both Malcolm's parents were good, pious people. He cannot understand why he is not, and he sadly bids Malcolm farewell. There is no point in his returning to Scotland. Indeed, there is no point in hoping any more.

Malcolm is moved. Macduff's loyalty to his country is clear and deep, and Malcolm tells him that this quality has wiped the evil from his own soul. He declares that Macbeth has tried to win him over by promising to sate the evil appetites he claimed he has. He has not succumbed. In the sight of God, young Malcolm puts himself under the older man's guidance and says that the vices he confessed he revelled in are complete strangers to him. He is a virgin; he has never lied; he has not coveted his neighbours' goods. He has always been honest. The picture of himself as a wicked man was the first lie he ever told (and that, of course, was to test Macduff). Again we see the theme of illusion and reality, but this time, most importantly, it acts for good. Malcolm *seems* a villain but is in fact a hero. In his true, virtuous self, Malcolm gives himself to Macduff and Scotland to command. Indeed, just as Macduff arrived, Old Siward with ten thousand armed men was about to set off to fight. Now they will all go together, hoping that the chance of success matches the value of their cause.

Macduff, not surprisingly, is confused ('Such welcome and un-welcome things at once/'Tis hard to reconcile'); but at this moment a Doctor enters to tell how many sick people are waiting for Edward the Confessor to heal them of the King's Evil. This illness is such that doctors cannot cure it. Only the virtuous king has been given the power to do so. People who are horribly afflicted come to him and he cures them by hanging a golden medal round their necks while uttering prayers. This magical, holy power is the hereditary gift of the kings of England. Edward can also prophesy. Such blessings as these show him indeed to be a king loved of God and full of grace.

The purpose of this brief interlude is threefold: to show what a truly good king should be, in contrast to Macbeth; to show the moral goodness that goes with Malcolm's troops (they have Edward's blessing); and to show James I the magical powers for good vested in the kings of England. (See pp. 80–82.)

Ross now enters and the final part of Macduff's testing takes place. He reports the violence and suffering that are Scotland's lot. There is a new grief every minute.

Macduff asks how his wife and children are. He is told briefly that they are 'well'. (They are so because they are dead.) They are indeed 'at peace'. Macduff begs for more details but Ross changes the subject: Macbeth is preparing for war, so the certain rumour goes, and now is the time for action. He turns to Malcolm and says that his mere presence in Scotland will create soldiers, and even the women would fight.

Malcolm tells him to be comforted. He is coming with the forces of the great Siward. ('An older and a better soldier none/That Christendom gives out').

It is then that Ross turns to Macduff. He cannot give him good news; rather, he says, he has words that should be howled out in the desert air. Do his words concern everyone, Macduff asks, or just a single person? Everyone, he is told, will feel sympathy, but the true tragedy is his alone. Macduff begs Ross to tell him quickly, though he already guesses what he has to say. When he is told of the murder of his wife and children he collapses with grief. It is left to Malcolm to comfort him, to urge him to speak, but Macduff is capable only of the broken sentences of true grief. Malcolm urges him to turn his desire for revenge to the good of his country, to summon it up as a special strength against Macbeth. As Macduff in his suffering replies: 'He has no children.' He declares that he must feel his sorrow as fully as a man can. Why did heaven not intervene? Again Malcolm urges him to use his grief and anger as 'the whetstone of your sword'. We see here how Malcolm, sympathetic as he is, is always aware of political significance. He is right to be so. Macduff does indeed come to use his fury against Macbeth: he wants to meet him in single combat. He will.

Malcolm is well pleased. His troops are loyal, brave, and have a true and deep motivation to fight. Now is the time to dethrone Macbeth. He is 'ripe for shaking'. Calling on heaven for help, Malcolm bids Macduff be as cheerful as he can. The long night that Macbeth has brought to Scotland cannot last for ever.

ACT V SCENE i

We watch the tragic ruin of Lady Macbeth. The terrifying woman whom we saw trying to transform herself into a monster and thinking that conscience was the hallmark of a coward is now a pathetic, mad creature broken by the strain of guilt. She has played with appearance and reality but has discovered, too late, that the reality of life is natural behaviour, loyalty and pity. Her suffering is a seemingly end-less repetition of the memories of guilt.

The Doctor has watched two nights with the Gentlewoman but has so far failed to see the sleepwalking Lady Macbeth. This, of course, serves to heighten the air of expectancy.

We learn in passing from the Gentlewoman that Macbeth has now prepared for war and that since he left the Gentlewoman has seen Lady Macbeth rise from her bed, dress, write on a secret paper, seal it and return to bed. During all this she has, it seems, been asleep. Such compulsive activity points to Lady Macbeth's deeply troubled state, a state made worse by an appearance of sleep from which she derives none of the benefits of rest. We are pitifully reminded that sleep has been denied to Macbeth and his wife since the time of the murder of Duncan.

The Gentlewoman also makes it clear that Lady Macbeth talks while she acts in this way, but she refuses, with a touching loyalty, to reveal to the Doctor the dreadful things she has heard.

At this point Lady Macbeth enters. This is one of the great moments of the English theatre; at once strange and deeply moving. We have seen how evil Lady Macbeth can be, but being presented with her collapse and suffering we are strangely moved to pity. It is precisely in this (and we shall see it again in Macbeth himself) that the tragic effect of the play lies. We are too moved to dismiss this woman as purely evil. Her wickedness and now her suffering inspire in us pity and terror.

Lady Macbeth compulsively rubs her hands. How easy murder had seemed to her when she had chided her husband with 'a little water clears us of this deed'. He knew that this was not the case. Such knowledge is part of the grandeur of his suffering. Now his wife discovers the same truth in her ceaseless attempts to remove the 'spot' of blood, the hallucinatory sign of her all too real guilt.

As she speaks (in prose, as is always the case with Shakespearian characters driven over the edge of reason) we hear pathetic echoes and quotations from her once furious defiance of conscience, the ever more demanding and exhausting face she had to put on the demands of decency. She cannot, in her madness, tell her story in a consecutive, coherent way. As she is forced to look back at the broken fragments of her past, it is as if she looks upon herself in a shattered mirror. The sharp edge of each memory lacerates her mind. She remembers chiding her husband, the great quantity of blood in Duncan's body, the reports she heard of the murder of Lady Macduff, and then, looking down, she sees her perpetually bloody hands.

The Doctor, professional man though he is, is deeply moved by her suffering, and the Gentlewoman hints again at her guilt. The Doctor, admitting he can do nothing for her in her madness and isolation, hears her as she speaks of Banquo and the arrival of the ghost at the feast. As the lingering echo of the knocking at the gate rings round her imagination, Lady Macbeth makes her way back to bed. The exhaustion of a restless conscience will eventually be too much for her. She has cut herself off from heaven; she is locked in her own insanity. She will be driven to despair, and finally, it seems, to suicide. Suicide, the murder of herself, is the only respite from her tortured conscience after the murder of Duncan.

The Doctor links Lady Macbeth's suspicious mutterings to general public gossip. Lady Macbeth, he says, needs a priest rather than a doctor. He bids the Gentlewoman keep Lady Macbeth safe, and with that he leaves. His last lines make it reasonably clear that he has understood her only too well.

ACT V SCENE ii

If *Macbeth* is a play about evil, the nature of evil and how evil finally leads to its own destruction, it is also a play about the positive and redeeming power of good and good intentions. We learn now from Menteith that the English army under Malcolm is near by. They are burning for revenge and their cause is so good, so righteous, that even dead men would be brought to life by it. Indeed, it is precisely this power of new life that Malcolm's youthful army promises. We learn that the forces are to meet near Birnan Wood (thus reminding us, perhaps, of the Third Apparition's prophecy) and that Macbeth has fortified his castle at Dunsinane.

Some people say he is mad, others (who are not so completely his enemies) call his mood 'valiant fury'. It is clear, however, that he is no longer wholly ruled by his reason. Just as the evil of Lady Macbeth will end in madness and death, so in its way will that of Macbeth himself. He has been driven to near insanity, as Angus declares, by his guilt, by the blood on his hands.

The Scottish army marches on to meet the English, confident that they are the true healers of their country's ills.

ACT V SCENE iii

As the scene opens, we see Macbeth again. The last occasion on which we saw him (IV, i) was some while ago when he encountered the Witches for the last, disastrous time. We saw then that madness, a homicidal mania, a refusal to listen to the promptings of reason, had possessed him. Hecate had intended this. Since that time, all we have heard of him has been by report, a report of continuous and ever more bloody murder and injustice.

His trust is now wholly and pathetically in the promises that seem to be held out to him by the Apparitions: that he cannot be harmed until Birnan Wood marches on his castle, that no man born of woman can ever kill him. Both these prophecies seem promises of security. The natural world would appear, at first sight, to have to change radically before woods can move or men of the promised type appear. Macbeth's trust is pathetic. He still believes and desperately clings to the entirely mistaken idea that what has been told him has been told him for his own good. Macbeth has put his trust in evil forces, unaware that they cannot of their very nature mean him good. He does not recognize how ambiguous their prophecies really are. The things that can never happen, the things that are indeed the desperate pledge of his security, *will* come to pass: Birnan Wood will move, Macbeth will encounter in Macduff a man not 'of woman born'. It is a particular irony of the Witches' prophecies that they always come true. From this moment until his death we shall see Macbeth slowly stripped of these last vestiges of security and finally destroyed.

The borderline between madness and 'valiant fury' is a fine one. Macbeth is far from settled and calm. The fear his servant shows rouses him to yet greater fury but this subsides almost at once into pessimism, even self-pity. Macbeth knows that the battle to be fought today will be the deciding one, but he knows too that he has lived long enough. The endless and increasingly bloody activity he has been bound to sustain in order to remain king has left him exhausted. Like a yellow autumn leaf, it is time for him to fall and die. There is nothing for him to live for. He has aged rapidly, but the good things that should go with old age, 'honour, love, obedience, troops of friends', he cannot have. His lot is the suspicion and hatred of those who surround him.

And in this pathos, in the remaining nobility of an all but exhausted mind that can express so beautifully, so poignantly, the futility of its own existence, lies the very power by which Macbeth is redeemed: redeemed for us as a tragic hero. We cannot wholly admire him. We have seen too much of his wickedness. But we cannot dismiss him as purely evil. There is a sad and terrible grandeur underlying the cornered, madly violent Macbeth of these last scenes. In this lies his stature as a tragic hero.

As a final irony, Macbeth rouses himself to fight. At the start of the play he was a great, loyal, blood-soaked soldier. Later we have seen the man of action almost paralysed by conscience, we have seen ambition get the better of conscience and so spur him to the most evil of actions.

We have seen, too, how one tremendous, sacrilegious letting of blood has had to be followed by much more. Now, at the end of the play, this heroic war machine of the first Act goes out again into the field of battle. There is a curious and moving mixture of glory and evil in this last defiance. Macbeth learns from the Doctor (who reappears at this point) that normal medicine cannot cure 'a mind diseased'. Macbeth realizes that just as medicine is useless for his wife, so it is for him. What drug, he asks, can remove the English forces? None. Macbeth himself is the illness and the forces of the young men know that it is they who are the true doctors to their country. There is no medicine for Macbeth beyond action, fighting. Macbeth summons up once again the supposed power and comfort of the Witches, but the Doctor, who has the last word in the scene, lets us know that he thinks Macbeth to be almost as desperate as his wife.

ACT V SCENE i v

Malcolm, addressing the leaders of his army, assures them that he is bringing peace to Scotland. He is a young, good and practical man. He knows the advantages of camouflage in hiding an army from the observation of the enemy and he orders each of the soldiers to hew down a branch from the trees of Birnan Wood. In this way they can march under cover. It will seem, of course, that the wood itself is moving. The order will fulfil the Apparition's prophecy. The prediction will come true. It was never intended as well meant towards Macbeth. He has trusted in the impossible idea of the powers of evil intending his good. The true forces of good are now on the march. They are well prepared and trained as they advance for battle.

ACT V SCENE v

Macbeth is increasingly desperate. He boasts of the strength of his castle but reports that many of his troops have gone over to the enemy. This adds to the sense of Macbeth's failing power. It will also explain why Dunsinane, apparently so strong, very quickly falls to Malcolm.

But within the castle there is pain. We hear the cry of women, unexplained as yet, but terrible and nerve-racking. Macbeth's response shows his exhaustion. There was a time when such a noise would have frightened him: now, as he declares, he has 'supped full with horrors'. Dreadful things are so commonplace to him that they no longer affect him.

The meaning of the cry is then explained to him: Lady Macbeth is dead.

Macbeth's isolation and exhaustion are complete, and his soliloquy here is the most potent of all his expressions of life's pointlessness: day succeeds petty day, our experience means nothing and points only to our death. The speech continues with powerful imagery: life is a candle that will gutter out, an actor who has his time on the stage and then, when he leaves it, is heard no more. Life is an idiot's tale, 'full of sound and fury, /Signifying nothing'. The speech is a very great and a famous one. Nearly every phrase in it is still used for common quotation, but its power remains undiminished. It is a masterpiece expressing total futility. In its exhaustion, its pathos, lies the poetic greatness that all but redeems Macbeth here at his desperate end.

That end comes very fast. His troops are deserting. Horror can no longer move him; he is alone without his wife and knows that existence is pointless. Now, as the Messenger comes in to give him news, we see the 'good' prophecies of the Witches turning to yet more causes for despair. The Messenger has seen Malcolm's camouflaged troops. To him it seems that Birnan Wood is on the move. The impossible has become possible: Birnan Wood is indeed moving. In a new panic, Macbeth turns on the Messenger and declares he will hang him if he is lying; if he is telling the truth, 'I care not if thou dost for me as much'.

At last Macbeth begins to recognize the 'equivocation' in the prophecies. Finally he understands that the powers of evil do not wish him well. To be sure, their prophecies are coming true, but in coming true they bring only Macbeth's destruction. The *appearance* of safety gives way to the *reality* of defeat. At the end of his speech Macbeth is torn between violent activity and a total indifference to whether he lives or dies.

ACT V SCENE vi

Malcolm orders his troops to put off their camouflage. Siward and his son are told to lead the troops into battle, while Malcolm and Macduff will effect 'what else remains to do'. The trumpets, 'those clamorous harbingers of blood and death', ring out.

Shakespeare presents the battle as a series of fast, brief and noisy encounters. We see Macbeth like a bear tied to a stake but still holding to the last of the prophecies: he cannot be hurt by a man born of woman. Young Siward enters. They fight, and the boy is slain. For a moment, Macbeth is triumphant. The last prophecy does indeed seem to work to his protection.

We glimpse Macduff, determined to fight Macbeth in the single combat he promised himself in Act IV Scene iii. The ghosts of his family will haunt his conscience if he does not kill the tyrant himself. He cannot fight mere mercenaries. He must fight Macbeth or no one, and he rushes into the thick of the battle to find him.

The energy, violence and speed that Shakespeare creates here are tremendous, but we should note how each section is designed to reflect on Macbeth. We learn now from old Siward that Dunsinane has fallen, that of Macbeth's vassals some are fighting for their lord and others against him. Malcolm's army is fighting well and the day is almost theirs. Malcolm, the future king, enters his enemy's castle. Victory is assured and all that we can expect now is the final defeat of Macbeth himself.

This takes place. Macduff encounters him, crying out, 'Turn, hell-hound, turn!' Macbeth turns, sees who is challenging him and confesses that he has avoided Macduff, of all men, because of the particularly savage destruction he has wreaked on Macduff's family. But Macduff has no time to bandy words: 'My voice is in my sword.' He wants action, rightful revenge. Macbeth pondered long before killing his king; Macduff needs no thought before killing this tyrant. They skirmish, but we should imagine Macduff at first getting the worst of it. Macbeth declares that it is pointless to fight him. He bears a 'charmèd life', and he explains why this should be so. But the last of the prophecies is no sooner mentioned than the hope it once implied is dashed. Macduff points out that he is not 'one of woman born'; rather was he 'from his mother's womb/Untimely ripped'. Macbeth now has nothing left to rely on but the strength of his arm. He is 'cowed' and finally, almost at the point of death, realizes that the Witches and their spirits appear to say one thing although they actually mean another. The Witches are the great equivocators who allow men to misinterpret what they say and so lead them to destruction, to the self-destruction of the evil man. Macduff calls on Macbeth to surrender; he will then be exposed to public humiliation: 'And live to be the show and gaze o' th' time'.

This is more than Macbeth can stand. He cannot accept humiliation. In a last desperate attempt, with the Witches' words revealed for what they are, he fights. He is the warrior to the end, the fighter going to certain death. Some moments later he is slain.

The victorious troops gather. Very few have been killed, chief among them being Young Siward who has died the death of a hero and is honoured accordingly. Bravely, even proudly, his father accepts this.

Macduff enters with Macbeth's severed head. Right at the start of the play, Macbeth, the loyal hero and soldier, had beheaded his king's enemy. Now the wheel has come full circle. Macbeth the traitor has, in his turn, been beheaded. Macduff hails Malcolm as the new king. The united forces all cheer him. Malcolm, secure in his new power, promises to reward their loyalty, and, as a special honour, creates earldoms for the Thanes. In due course he will call home loyal exiles and seek out Macbeth's former allies. We learn, merely by the way, that Lady Macbeth, the 'fiend-like queen', has probably committed suicide. She and her 'butcher' husband are safely out of the way. The play ends with Malcolm thanking the nobles who have supported him, and inviting them to see him crowned at Scone.

Characters

MACBETH

Macbeth is a tragic hero: a man whose enormous powers of body and mind are perverted to evil. The dreadful nature of this evil and the suffering it so movingly causes him are both terrifying and pitiful. In this lies Macbeth's tragic stature.

Shakespeare does not present us with his hero directly. The Witches appear first, and with them the powerful suggestion of an evil which has singled Macbeth out. From the start we sense that Macbeth is concerned in evil, marked out by forces over which he has no control. But Shakespeare is also concerned to present us with something else, something contradictory: Macbeth as the loyal subject of his king, the mighty soldier, the man of action, the war machine. This is the great man who will fall, and the speeches of the 'bleeding Captain' are most important in this respect. They build up the picture of the true hero, the man at once loyal and brave.

The kingdom of Scotland is threatened by a two-pronged rebellion. The enemy forces under Macdonwald are very nearly successful. It is 'brave Macbeth' (you should notice that this is the first description of him) who routs them, cutting a passage through them and killing Macdonwald. So we first hear of Macbeth as a loyal man of action, a man covered in the blood of his country's enemies. The Captain describes how Macbeth cuts off Macdonwald's head and fixes it on the battlements. But this is not the end of the matter. The Norwegian forces seize their advantage and Macbeth, with Banquo, routs them as well. This is a particularly bloody battle but Ross confirms that Macbeth has again been victorious. Macbeth is a worthy bridegroom for the goddess of war and it seems his actual presence on the battlefield has been crucial on each occasion. The King, as a mark of special favour, gives Macbeth the title of a traitor shortly to be executed for aid given to the Norwegians: he creates him Thane of Cawdor.

These speeches not only build up the picture of a hero; they deepen the irony of the play. The description of Macbeth is of a man of blood — so far, blood shed in his country's cause. This violence, however, will be terrible when turned on his king. We see here a man of action and decision: soon we shall see a man paralysed by doubt. Macbeth is given the title Thane of Cawdor. The loyal man is given the title of a traitor, but soon Macbeth will show himself to be a more dangerous traitor than Cawdor himself. In a final irony, everybody except Macbeth and Banquo know he has received the honour. It is only after he has met the Witches that he will be told of it. By then it will not be a well-deserved gift, but almost certain proof that he will become king. The Witches' prophecies will indeed be fulfilled.

Macbeth himself is not introduced until we have seen the Witches for a second time. The First Witch's treatment of the master of the *Tiger* is a foretaste of what will happen to Macbeth, but the very presence of the Witches reinforces the idea of the evil Macbeth is courting. His first words, when we finally see him, are deeply ambiguous: the day is 'foul' because of the storm (caused by the Witches) and 'fair' because of the victory. Matters seem to be in exact balance. From now on evil will predominate. The evil will be caused (see pp. 82–5) by men and women labouring to bring the Witches' prophecies true. For the moment the Witches simply stop Macbeth and greet him with three titles: one he has inherited legitimately from his father, another he has just been given (again legitimately) by his king, the third he commits murder to acquire. At this point it is vital to imagine the effect of the play on stage. When he has heard the Witches, Macbeth is plunged into profound and silent thought. No longer the man of action, we see the possibility of evil sinking down through his mind. He tries to ask where the Witches come from and why they have singled him out, but they vanish and the origins and purposes of evil remain obscure.

But it is now — immediately — that the first of their prophecies comes true. Macbeth is told that he has been made Thane of Cawdor. He is careful to question this news but, on its confirmation, he is plunged again into thought. He now believes in the prophecy of kingship and, as his companions talk, he is left alone, muttering his thoughts in soliloquy. His words are full of doubt and ambiguity. What the Witches have said is good in so far as it has been fulfilled by his new title, bad in so far as his imagination is now working on the thought of the murder of his king, the king for whom he has recently shown himself to be so brave a soldier.

This muttering, suspicious man is a very changed creature indeed. The reality is now very different from the appearance of heroism. Macbeth is locked in a private world of thought, a private world that will become ever more claustrophic. For the moment, though, we are left with one great, final doubt: will this man commit the murder which so appals him? When Macbeth encounters the King and receives his praise he tells Duncan, in words that are wholly appropriate, that he has done no more than a loyal subject should (I, iv, lines 23–8). But the division between appearance and reality – the appearance of bravery and the reality of treason – is made even more obvious by his realization that when Duncan has appointed Malcolm heir to the throne there is another barrier in his way. The power of the evil images he summons up in the soliloquy at the end of Act I Scene iv shows how clearly and rapidly Macbeth has become associated with evil.

But Macbeth is not yet wholly committed to the powers of darkness. He still has noble feelings, and he realizes the gravity of what he is proposing. His wife feels that such scruples are mere cowardice. She dwells on what she calls Macbeth's weakness (I, v) and, summoning up within herself forces of wholly unnatural evil, prepares to drive Macbeth towards the fulfilment of the third of the Witches' prophecies. She will chide his cowardice and will tell Macbeth that he is not a man; he will be forced nearer the murder not only by his own inclination but also by his wife's accusation of inadequacy. We feel very strongly the power of the forces pitted against Macbeth.

That Macbeth is still not committed to the immediate murder of Duncan is made clear when his wife sees and forces the advantage of Duncan's stay in their castle. Macbeth tries to dissuade her but to no avail. By the time we see him again he has gone far and fast along an evil road. We are shown how self-destructive his course of action proves to be.

Act I Scene vii starts with a great soliloquy: a speech from a man both on his own and endlessly divided against himself. What is so fascinating and so moving about this speech is the way in which it reveals the doubtful progress of a once great but now increasingly paralysed man of action towards a deed whose wickedness and danger he fully recognizes. Macbeth knows that the murder of his king will ensure his damnation and he is (quite rightly) afraid of the inevitable punishment. What remains of the man of honour knows that as Duncan's host and vassal he is the last man who should kill him. Duncan is not only his king appointed by God and his murder is therefore a sacrilege, he is also so good a man that his murder will seem particularly evil. Macbeth realizes that he has nothing to spur him on to this evil deed but his own ambition. That ambition, fed by Lady Macbeth, will be all he needs. The root of Macbeth's desire is very simple: its effects and repercussions, as he knows, will not only be complex, they will also be on an enormous scale. The greatness, fascination and tragedy of Macbeth lies precisely in the fact that he is aware of the issues involved.

Nevertheless, for the moment he tries to stop it all. This is his very last chance of safety. He loses it. He is told by his wife he is less than a man, a coward. She awes him into an acceptance of her own evil. Its power seems to reassure Macbeth, to take away the fear, the doubt that might have saved him. Seeking a solution to his own doubts, he finds one in the apparent strength of Lady Macbeth. Against the rule of nature the man is led by his wife, led by her to his destruction. But he is led by a ruthlessness which is more illusion than reality. Lady Macbeth is not nearly as strong as she appears. They will both discover (with tragic effect) the consequences of this moment of decision when neither of them is acting in accord with their true nature.

When Macbeth encounters Banquo (II, i) it becomes clear that the very thought of murder leads him to deal falsely with his friends, to set up a long chain of double-dealing and suspicion which will eventually wear him out. His tension is so great that he moves into hallucination. He sees floating before him the dagger with which he is to murder Duncan. He doubts whether it is real or simply an illusion. His soliloquy is one of the greatest dramatic vividness, exciting us into sympathy with Macbeth's state of fevered imagination. But as he dismisses the vision as an illusion and summons up images of evil almost as if they were a spell (associating himself ever more clearly with evil), so we see the man poised on the point of incredible wickedness. He is anxious to get on with the deed now and the bell summons him to it.

Let us sum up what we know about this man who is about to kill his king. He is a man of great character who is tempted into evil. He has tried to resist this evil because he is aware of its implications. From being the noble and loyal man of action he has become a creature tortured by his conscience. He has tried to repress his ambition, but its strength, coupled with the persuasion of his wife, has got the better of him. We have been moved by his efforts to resist evil and excited by his temptation. We have watched as the forces are stacked against him. We have seen the rapid corruption of a hero. With his entry into the bedroom and Duncan's murder the first phase in the development of Macbeth's character is over.

Macbeth returns to his wife, a trembling, suspicious and all but hysterical man. In the way he behaves, in his fear and nervousness, the tremendous significance of the murder of a king is demonstrated. We do not need to be shown the murder itself. It is far more convincing, far more dramatically compelling, that we are shown the effect on Macbeth, the utter destruction of his peace of mind, his awareness that he has been cut off from God and from natural rest. We know that from now on Macbeth will be on his own. So does he. Evil he is, and more evil he will become. It is the depth of his suffering and his awareness of its implications that make Macbeth so profoundly moving: a tragic hero. It is not usual to be impressed by murderers, particularly murderers who have killed in Macbeth's cowardly way. But because of the greatness of his mind, the power of the poetry he speaks, we are indeed truly impressed. Macbeth is both frightened and aware that he will never be clean again, that he is damned. The knocking at the gate (the almost immediate arrival of the forces of good) makes him shout out in desperation. From now on, his will be a role of increasing horror.

Macbeth has made his castle a hell on earth. The 'Porter scene' makes this clear. In this self-made hell Macbeth is doomed to the practice of continual deception. At first he is quite adept, greeting

Macduff and Lennox as if nothing had happened, but when (II, iii, ll. 88–93) he publicly declares (as he must) that the meaning has gone out of life with the murder of Duncan, we feel the tragedy of the private significance of his comment. Such a world – futile, graceless, bitter – Macbeth is now doomed to explore. This is the second stage in the development of his character: Macbeth confronted by continual suspicion and fear. These will wear him down until in desperation he returns to the Witches. Then he will be driven mad.

With the arrival of Macduff and Lennox, Macbeth already has to shed more blood: the blood of the grooms. He has to kill them to preserve his alibi. He has to state publicly his reason for killing them. This double murder is the first of many more Macbeth must commit in the vain attempt to keep himself from the consequences of the murder of his king. He has unleashed bloodshed and chaos in nature and the whole of Scotland. We see the pathetic, trapped Macbeth, for whom a third murder, that of Banquo, has now become a necessity. As Macbeth questions Banquo about his ride and at the same time invites him to the feast that night, we are shown how accomplished and ruthless Macbeth's lying has become. Banquo suspects nothing and Macbeth gets from him the necessary information about the ride while successfully eliminating any suspicion of himself. But the agonizing self-questioning that underlies the murder is clear in the following soliloquy (III, i, ll. 47–71). Banquo is loyal, brave, good and therefore a danger. He has, crucially, been hailed as father to a line of kings. This particular prophecy has not so far played an important part in Macbeth's thought. Now it obsesses him. The repercussions of the murder of Duncan are far more complex than at first they seemed. Macbeth is fully aware of his dilemma. If Banquo's descendants become kings, Macbeth has given his soul to damnation for nothing. He has not even an earthly reward which is secure. Cut off from heaven and denied glory in this world, his state must be futile, meaningless; a suffering without end and to no purpose. The realization of this creates in him a depth and pathos which are tragic.

With great skill, Macbeth whets the Murderers' appetites (III, i, ll. 73–139) and we notice something that adds yet another dimension of futility to Macbeth's position: a new dimension of futility and of pathos. Macbeth believes he can control fate, his own fate. Having set in motion the machinery by which the prophecies of the Witches will come true, he thinks he can then tamper with things, and alter or deny the rest of their prophecies. He believes he can murder Banquo and Fleance and so secure the throne for his own children. He cannot. Act III Scene ii shows that the fears Macbeth and his wife suffer are exhausting. Macbeth, pitifully confident in his false belief that he can manipulate his destiny, has taken the initiative in evil from his wife. His speech at the end of this scene makes his pleasure in this clear. It also associates him powerfully with the forces of evil – forces which will prevent his happiness in the world.

That he is not the master of his fate is almost immediately demonstrated. The murder is bungled. Banquo is killed, but Fleance escapes to fulfil the prophecy and Macbeth is again thrown into an agony of claustrophobic horror (III, iv, ll. 20–25). But this suffering is nothing compared with the terror that comes to Macbeth when the ghost of Banquo takes its place at the feast. Not only has Macbeth failed to control his fate, he is now haunted (privately and alone) by a world of ghosts whose existence he had not even suspected. Far worse than the hallucination of the dagger, this ghostly visitation drives Macbeth to the edge of sanity and the realization that, as a mere man, he cannot compete with the spiritual world (III, iv, ll. 98–106). Events are now out of his control. But, to add to his doubts, Lady Macbeth realizes that Macduff did not come to the feast. What does this mean? The doubts proliferate. Macbeth has a world of anguishing problems to solve. Not only has he been denied sleep, but the whole of his waking life is agonizingly filled with one problem after another, each requiring a bloody solution.

Macbeth will soon discover the reason for Macduff's absence. To be sure, we have been deeply moved by Macbeth's plight, by the increasing panic that is wearing down this once noble man, driving him to near insanity. We have been moved by such suffering, but we are not allowed to forget that Macbeth is a profoundly evil man: a tyrant. We are therefore both sympathetic towards him and repelled by him. This, like everything else in the play, is deeply ambiguous. Macbeth's tyranny is thoroughly modern. He keeps himself informed by the use of double agents (III, iv, ll. 130–31). But these merely mortal spies are not enough. The exhausted Macbeth must go to the Witches and force further knowledge from them. We are then shown the Witches again (III, v). They are resolved to drive Macbeth to madness. Hecate declares that she will deprive Macbeth of 'security': that is, she will take away from him all reasonable fear. She will drive him to a madness of bloody homicide.

The visit to the Witches is a remarkable scene (IV, i). We know what is going to happen. Hecate has already told us that Macbeth will be driven mad. We know when he comes in, determined to force from the Witches some certainty about his future, that he is not in control, and this seems an added dimension to his suffering. He is ignorant of the vast magical forces lined up against him. He is determined to learn his fate. He is both abusive and wordy – a man desperately and arrogantly assuming that he can control his destiny. The words of the Witches rapidly deflate him; they could not answer his demands more simply and the anticlimax is particularly humiliating. Not only are Macbeth's forceful words redundant, but he is told to sit still and merely to listen. When the First Apparition appears, Macbeth speaks to it but is told not only that it already knows his thoughts, but that he is to keep silent. He, who came vowing to discover his fate, could hardly be made more helpless: effectively, he is told to shut up and listen.

The three Apparitions tell him to beware Macduff; that he need fear 'none of woman born'; and that he is safe until Birnam Wood marches against his castle. As always, the Witches speak the truth and their prophecies will come true – but in ways that Macbeth could not possibly have expected. The first speech confirms his own intuition of the danger from Macduff, but the second and third prophecies seem to argue Macbeth's complete safety. He can, for a few moments, be gloriously confident (IV, i, ll. 93–9). He is wholly unaware (master of duplicity though he has become) that the Witches are the greatest of equivocators, that everything spoken by them or by their Apparitions has a double meaning.

The reassurance that seems to be offered by the second and third prophecies is not enough for Macbeth. He is desperately worried. The fear that Banquo's descendants will inherit the throne still troubles him, for if they do succeed, of course, he has murdered for nothing. Macbeth must, then, press the Witches for a clear and unambiguous answer. He is warned not to ask, but he insists. What he is shown will, as the Witches know, 'grieve his heart' and drive him, as they intend, over the brink of reason. A dumb-show of eight kings passes across the stage, wordless but cruelly certain in their message that the Witches' prophecy to Banquo will indeed come true: 'Thou shalt get kings, though thou be none.' The tormented Macbeth (and we sympathize with his horror and his suffering) begs to be told that this is not so. The Witches, however, only tell the truth. They have no sympathy. They grossly try to entertain the horrified Macbeth with a dance, and then disappear. He is left with the realization of his horrible state: he has destroyed his life and soul for nothing. Banquo's issue will reign over the kingdom, and Macbeth must pay the price of Duncan's murder without reward. It is his realization that this is so which makes him deeply moving, villain though he is. This villainy now turns to madness. Macbeth says that he will do the first, the bloodiest things that come to mind, whatever the consequences. He will fulfil Hecate's prophecy that he will go mad. With a mindless brutality which all but destroys our pity for him, Macbeth vows to slaughter Macduff's wife, his children and his relations. His bloodthirsty tyranny is absolute. At this point he is not to be pitied – he is obscene. He is a homicidal tyrant in the mould of Hitler and Stalin. The anguish of Lady Macduff and her son as they talk and are then slaughtered (IV, ii) makes this perfectly clear.

From Act III Scene vi we have learned that life under a tyrant such as Macbeth is a life of hints, guesses, and unanswered questions. In Act IV Scene iii (the long scene, set in England, which presents Malcolm as the only hope for Scotland) we learn of the reign of terror that Macbeth has unleashed on Scotland. The reports of Macduff and Ross are those of observers in any tyranny: reports of a welter of blood and anguish. With these descriptions of mindless brutality the second stage of Macbeth's character development ends. Our sympathy for him stands at its lowest point. His cruelty is almost beyond our understanding.

It is an essential element in the greatness of *Macbeth* that Shakespeare can revive our sympathy; despite such wickedness as we have heard reported (or, in fact, seen) we can return to a view of Macbeth which is not wholly sympathetic but at least contains a deal of pity. Out of the appalling bloodshed, the tyranny, the sheer human unhappiness that Macbeth has so eagerly created, Shakespeare can make a man who is a tragic hero. This is the last part of Macbeth's development. Through the sheer power of his poetry, his sense of the pointlessness of life, Shakespeare creates a man who strikes us with both pity and awe. In this play about ambiguity, Macbeth remains a profoundly ambiguous figure.

When we see Macbeth again (V, iii) he is a cornered, desperate man surrounded by the forces of good and mumbling the prophecies of the Apparitions as if they were magic charms devised for his own safety. The pace of the action and the desperation of those who surround him, however, show us a Macbeth on the tragic edge of despair. He is fighting out of defiance, like a cornered animal. But Macbeth is more than bestial, his sure and poetic grip on the fact that his life is useless to him is deeply moving. All of us, at one time or another, may feel that our lives are not worth living. Macbeth voices this despair. His life *is* pointless. He destroyed its meaning when he destroyed Duncan, when he ceased to be the loyal subject of the King. None of the good things – honour, love, friendship – will be there to support him through his old age. He feels that he should fall and rot like a dead leaf. This deep pessimism is most evident when he is told that his wife is dead. In his grief (for he can still feel grief) he breaks out into perhaps the greatest of his soliloquies (V, v, ll. 17–28). There is a difference between this profound despair and mere self-pity. Self-pity is sentimental and self-indulgent. Macbeth is neither of these things. What he says here is brutally true, and it is not said for effect. Unlike the self-pitier, he does not want anyone to help him. He knows that no one can. So, rather than passively waiting to die, Macbeth seizes the whole of life, of fate, and rouses himself to action: 'At least we'll die with harness on our back'. This is the cry of the soldier who has sold out on his loyalty. If Macbeth is vicious, which he undoubtedly is, he is also infinitely tragic in the way in which he rouses himself to active life. It is a rousing to action that can lead only to his death.

The end comes very quickly. One by one his hopes are stripped away: his wife dies, Birnan Wood is seen to move, his forces desert him, he is cornered in his castle, his castle falls. He is left alone, refusing suicide (V, vi, ll. 40–41), his wife's gesture of despair.

Macbeth now encounters Macduff, the one man he has sought to avoid, and they fight. We need to be particularly aware of the effect the play makes when it is performed on the stage. Macbeth at first seems to be winning. This is extraordinarily exciting: perhaps he is not quite a lost man. Flushed by his near victory, he calls out to Macduff the last of the Apparitions' prophecies: he cannot be harmed by a man born of woman. This charm is defiantly hurled at Macduff, for Macbeth wants to assure him that he has been promised supernatural safety. But Macduff, born by Caesarean section, is not a man born naturally by a woman's efforts. The last charm evaporates. With it, instantaneously, Macbeth's strength vanishes too. At last he realizes that the Witches are equivocators who have drawn down his soul to hell. He all but gives up. When Macduff tells him that only humiliation awaits him if he lives, Macbeth fights on to die, as he has lived, by the sword. This is a desperate, pathetic, truly tragic end: it makes us feel great pity for a man who has suffered so much, and awe that any human being could have been so crushed. At the start of the play we heard how Macbeth cut off a traitor's head; at the end, his own head is brought in as a symbol that evil has been destroyed.

LADY MACBETH

The Lady Macbeth we first encounter is an awesome woman: a self-made monster of evil and ambition. As the tragedy takes its course she dwindles under the effects of conscience until she is the pathetic, sleep-walking lunatic we see at the beginning of Act V. Right at the end of the play we hear (almost incidentally, as if it were a matter of no importance) that she has probably committed suicide. Any study of Lady Macbeth must follow this process of decline, despair and death.

It is Lady Macbeth who spurs her husband into fulfilling the

Witches' prophecies. When we first see her she is reading Macbeth's letter in which his meeting with them is described. She learns that the first prophecy – that Macbeth will be made Thane of Cawdor – has been almost immediately fulfilled. We have seen how appalled Macbeth is by the thought of the consequences of Duncan's murder. We have been moved by the almost irresistible temptation put in his way and the suffering it causes him. Now, in the first of her great soliloquies, Lady Macbeth reinforces these ideas. She knows that her husband, while ambitious, has feelings for what is right and what is wrong. In saying this she makes us realize that he is indeed a man. But for her purposes he is, as she says, 'too full o' the milk of human-kindness'. It is this she knows she must pervert if she is to have her way, if she is to be queen of Scotland. Her naked ambition appears at first much stronger than Macbeth's own. She seems to be a woman wholly without morals, a woman who believes that sheer willpower is the only important thing in the world. As she details Macbeth's weaknesses and describes how she will pour her 'spirits' in his ear, we have a growing impression of a monstrous evil and an iron will. What the Witches have predicted she will surely force into being. This appearance (and it *is* only an appearance) of total evil makes us realize that the already tempted Macbeth stands very little chance indeed of saving his soul from damnation.

It is when Lady Macbeth is told that Duncan is actually coming to the castle that night that we see her ambition and her wickedness grow and flourish. In her first soliloquy she spoke in worldly terms about the achievement of worldly ambition. Now, in her second soliloquy, she summons up her evil in the form of magic. Lady Macbeth wants to turn her nature into wholly unnatural channels. We have seen that she is more dominant and more ambitious than it was thought right for a woman to be; now Lady Macbeth no longer wishes to be a woman at all. She wants to be Evil personified, pitiless and iron-willed. In expressing this, she calls on the aid of magic powers, becoming in imagination a creature with the supernatural evil of the Witches themselves. Far from offering the 'milk of human-kindness', she wishes that her breasts were full of poison. She wants to be at one with magically 'murdering ministers'. At the close of this tremendous speech she summons up night, death and hell. The murderer's knife is already visible to her mind's eye. She wants to use it in the dark, secretly, out of the sight of heaven. By sheer force of words and willpower she appears to have re-created herself as a monster. It is terribly important that we, the audience, remember that in reality she is nothing more than a mortal woman, a woman who will suffer the pangs of guilt and conscience just like any other. She is not what she seems.

At this moment of great excitement, on seeing her husband she addresses him (as the Witches themselves addressed him) as Glamis, Cawdor and future king. She has imagined herself, willed herself, into monstrous evil. In her excited imagination and the strength of will this gives her, she takes her husband over. She will, she says, do 'this night's great business'. She is confident and, apparently, unshakeably strong. When Duncan arrives at the castle she triumphantly leads him inside and so to his death. But Lady Macbeth has constantly to reinforce her husband's resolve. In Act I Scene vii we find him wandering round the castle in an agony of doubt. When he sees his wife he tries to put a stop to the whole murder plan. She turns on him. She has tried to inspire him, but now she tries a different tactic; she, as a woman, will humiliate Macbeth as a man. She will call him a coward (you should recall that at the start of the play Macbeth was seen as a worthy bridegroom for the goddess of war herself) and so try to rouse his ambition that way.

Macbeth tries to silence her. He knows perfectly well that he is not a coward. He can do all the bravest man can do. He does not want to go further and become a monster. This is the truth. Lady Macbeth scorns it and says Macbeth was a real man when he hatched the murder plot. (You should note that he did not in fact devise this plan; the full details of it were Lady Macbeth's invention.) She adds that, since he wants to throw away the golden opportunity of Duncan's presence in the castle, he is a mere weakling. She, with the most grotesque image she can call up, says that she would dash the brains out of her baby rather than let this chance slip by. Her strength is irresistible. All that is left to Macbeth is to ask what will happen if they should fail. Lady Macbeth contemptuously declares this impossible, and outlines her plan: she will make the grooms drunk, she and her husband will then murder Duncan and the grooms will take the blame. The plan is a ruthlessly simple and cowardly one. It seems so safe. It confirms Macbeth's intention, although he knows it is wrong. In the moral weakness inspired by his ambition he has let his wife's iron will destroy his doubts. Lady Macbeth's *appearance* of total strength destroys the *reality* of her husband's conscience, his sophisticated moral sense.

Now, almost immediately, we see the flaws in this iron will. Lady Macbeth has given all the appearance of strength, now she begins the long and painful discovery of her reality as a weak woman. She cannot be wholly ruthless just because she wants to be. She cannot pretend that conscience and feelings do not exist. At the start of Act I I Scene ii we see her drinking to keep up her spirits, and we learn that for all her boasting, for all her apparent ruthlessness, she could not kill her king. The sleeping Duncan reminds her of her father and she falters.

But she is almost immediately confronted by her husband: 'I have done the deed,' Macbeth tells her. A man nearly broken by the murder, tense, frightened and aware that he is now cut off both from heaven and from natural sleep, Macbeth realizes the significance of what he has done. The pathos of Lady Macbeth lies in the strain she has to endure as she tries to brace her husband against his despair. His mind dwells on what he has done. As she says, in lines that tell us how the play will develop:

> *These deeds must not be thought*
> *After these ways; so, it will make us mad.*

Lady Macbeth tries to cope with her suffering husband in two ways: by being harsh, and by being practical. She tells her husband to go and wash the blood off his hands and then, seeing he has brought out the daggers, she summons up her courage to take them back to the chamber and so ensure their alibi. When she returns to hear the knocking at the gate, she is again practical. She decides they must put on their nightclothes so that it will seem that they have both been in bed all this while.

The arrival of Macduff marks the point at which the murder becomes a public event. Lady Macbeth's first public response when she is told of the murder is to faint. Whether this is a ploy, or whether she really faints from the strain of keeping up appearances, you must decide. Certainly, when we see her again, an important change has come over her relationship with Macbeth. She is no longer the dominant and planning partner. She asks Banquo to the feast that night, but she is unaware that Macbeth has planned to murder him. She knows that Banquo is a danger, but in Act III Scene ii, while she still realizes that she must keep Macbeth from despair, it is obvious that he has taken over from her. He does not tell her the details of his plan but hints at 'a deed of dreadful note'. When she asks him what this is she is not told. Macbeth merely (but with tremendous poetic power) summons up images of evil to amaze her. The self-created monster of Act I has lost the initiative in evil.

Lady Macbeth's behaviour at the feast (III, iv) shows the stress she is under. She is quiet at first and Macbeth (showing how their roles have been reversed) bids her welcome their guests. The First Murderer enters, and Macbeth's whispered, desperate conversation with him threatens to spoil the atmosphere of the feast, as Lady Macbeth points out. The appearance of Banquo's ghost and Macbeth's reaction to it entirely ruin the feast. Macbeth's hysteria is increased when it becomes clear that the ghost is visible only to him. Neither Lady Macbeth nor the guests can understand his terror. With quick-witted invention Lady Macbeth makes up an excuse: Macbeth has had this illness since his youth. It is nothing. They should take no notice of it. She tries her hardest to make him pull himself together, but to no effect. Lady Macbeth's last resort is to ask the guests not to question him and then, with a complete lack of ceremony, she tells them all to go home. She is left alone with her husband.

This is the last time we see them together. They are both in a state of extreme nervous exhaustion, particularly Lady Macbeth. She says very little, but we feel her almost desperate tiredness as she urges her still plotting husband to stop. His range of evil is beyond her. First a would-be monster, Lady Macbeth is now simply an exhausted woman. We shall not see her sane again.

Lady Macbeth does not appear in Act IV. This long absence makes her appearance as the mad, broken woman at the start of Act V all the more convincing. The reality of conscience, of human feeling, has reduced her to this pitiful state. She shuffles, sleep-walking, across the stage. She tries to rub an invisible spot of blood from her hand, and then, in the halting speech of the mad (for which Shakespeare uses prose, not verse), she goes over and over the guilty details of her past. She can no longer tell a connected story, but we feel each remembered incident lacerating her brain. Her sighs are dreadful. Eventually this restless agony will drive Lady Macbeth to despair. Almost at the close of the play (and almost as if it were a matter of no importance) we learn that she has probably committed suicide.

It is a pathetic end, but her story as a whole relates to the evil of the entire play. Lady Macbeth believed that she could be as evil as she wished. Ambition and worldly success were everything to her, and any degree of wickedness was justified for her in the pursuit of these ends. Conscience, she thought, was for cowards. She did not accept that evil is self-destructive. This she has to learn and this is what we are shown. The impression she gives of overpowering evil *is* only an impression. Her inability to murder Duncan is the first clue that human feeling is more powerful than naked ambition. As she gets to grips with the reality of evil, both hers and her husband's, we see the strain of keeping up appearances becoming intolerable. Restless guilt mounts in Lady Macbeth. She has to continue to support her husband, excuse him, and think about her own insecure future. All this finally breaks her. Even in her madness she is tortured. For her there is no escape from guilt except in death – her probable suicide. What makes her so compelling (as Macbeth himself is fascinating as a character) is Shakespeare's ability to make us pity her, evil though she is.

BANQUO

Banquo is a great soldier, second, indeed, only to Macbeth. At the start of the play we are told by Duncan (I, ii, ll. 33–4) that Banquo and Macbeth are the 'captains' of the forces fighting the rebels. When we first see Banquo it is as Macbeth's companion (I, iii). It is Banquo who seems to glimpse the Witches first and it is he who informs us of Macbeth's response. Banquo questions them about his own future but the Witches' replies are particularly ambiguous. He will be 'lesser than Macbeth, and greater', and 'not so happy, yet much happier'. He is also told: 'Thou shalt get kings, though thou be none.' As is always the case with the Witches' prophecies, these predictions come true. Banquo will not achieve Macbeth's position of king, but by preserving his integrity he will be the greater man. He will not murder (indeed, he will be murdered) but will be spared Macbeth's guilty suffering. The third prophecy, that he will be father to a line of kings, is vital in explaining Macbeth's subsequent fear of Banquo and the reason why he has to have him killed.

Banquo is far more suspicious of the Witches than Macbeth is, and he gives Macbeth a warning:

> ... *oftentimes, to win us to our harm,*
> *The instruments of darkness tell us truths;*
> *Win us with honest trifles, to betray's*
> *In deepest consequence.*

(I, iii, ll. 122–5)

This, of course, proves to be true.

It is Banquo, who is both brave and shrewd, who opens Act II, giving us the first necessary hint of suspicion. He serves as a foil to the increasingly two-faced Macbeth. Throughout, Banquo appears hard-headed and intelligent. He is loyal and a good subject. It is he who (II, iii), when the murder has been made public, suggests that all concerned should meet to discuss the consequences. He also guesses, quite rightly, that Macbeth has murdered his way to the throne (III, i). He realizes the wickedness of what Macbeth has done and that the prophecies have been fulfilled. Banquo does not lack worldly ambition; he merely disdains evil methods to achieve it.

In his soliloquy in Act III Scene i, however, Shakespeare makes Macbeth's reasons for wanting to be rid of Banquo perfectly clear. It is in praise of Banquo for his level-headedness and wisdom, but it also hints at a certain aura that makes Macbeth feel inadequate. As important, however, is the Witches' third prophecy to Banquo. Macbeth realizes that if Banquo's children do succeed to the throne, then he has murdered and sold his soul for nothing, and is suffering the pangs of conscience to no end. In the desperate attempt to secure safety, Banquo must be destroyed. At the beginning of the third Act, we see Macbeth questioning him and finding out the time and place he can have Banquo killed, the murder taking place in Act III Scene iii. The fact that it happens as Banquo is returning to Macbeth's castle for the feast only underlines the depths of deceit of which Macbeth is capable. The escape of Fleance, Banquo's son, confirms that the Witches' prophecy will be fulfilled. The bungled murder attempt shows he is not master of his fate. Neither is Macbeth master of his emotions. Banquo's last and most dramatic role is his ghostly appearance at the feast. The good and loyal man returns to haunt the private world of Macbeth's guilt. His closest friend becomes one of his cruellest tormentors.

MACDUFF

The character of Macduff echoes these themes of goodness and loyalty. Banquo is the good man who is destroyed by Macbeth's evil; Macduff is the good man who helps to vanquish it. The roles are complementary. It is Macduff who knocks on the gate of the castle immediately after Duncan's murder, thereby showing that goodness is never wholly absent from the world. It is Macduff who commands the alarm bell to be rung, thereby announcing to the world the murder of Duncan.

Likewise, it is he who makes clear (II, iv) that the alibi Macbeth and his wife have used for the murder has been publicly accepted – but, significantly, he does not attend Macbeth's coronation. It is likely that even at this point he has his suspicions. Certainly, he refuses to attend the banquet. If Macduff does indeed realize what has happened almost from the start, then we should imagine him speaking the alibi for the murder (II, iv) in the voice of a man telling something that most people believe to be true but which he can see through.

Macduff's failure to attend the feast rouses Macbeth's suspicions of him and perhaps furthers Macbeth's desperate need to consult the Witches again. We also learn a little later (III, vi) not only that he has refused Macbeth his help against the English but that he has actually gone to England himself. Macbeth does not know this yet, but for the audience it is a first indication of hope: a good and intelligent man is trying to do something about the tyranny under which Scotland has fallen.

When Macbeth finally returns to the Witches and is confronted by the images of his future, the First Apparition tells him:

> *Macbeth, Macbeth, Macbeth, beware Macduff!*
> *Beware the Thane of Fife!*

(I V, i, ll. 70–71)

It is immediately after this second meeting, when the Witches have driven him beyond reason, that Macbeth says he will act on impulse and do the first thing that comes into his head. He is told that Macduff has fled to England and his first idea is to slaughter Macduff's wife, family and relations. Macduff's flight to England is at once the promise of hope and the reason for Macbeth's most barbarous act.

Act I V Scene ii shows us this slaughter, but it is in the following scene that Macduff's importance in the play is fully developed. We see him in England and with Malcolm. It is Macduff, unaware of his personal tragedy, who tells Malcolm of the wholesale slaughter and tyranny that Macbeth has unleashed on Scotland. It is Macduff's loyalty that Malcolm is determined to test. Malcolm recognizes that he himself is a young man. He knows that if he is to be restored to his kingdom, then he will need Macduff's help. He knows, too, that he must be absolutely certain he can trust Macduff. Malcolm questions him very closely to discover whether Macduff is a double agent. When he is satisfied that he is not, he examines him further by presenting himself as a man even less capable of kingship than Macbeth. Macduff, wholly loyal to the legitimate heir to the throne, tries to make excuses for Malcolm. Only when, with the bitterest reluctance, he is obliged to admit that Malcolm does seem truly vicious and, indeed, not fit to live does Macduff's loyalty to his country appear most strongly. But no sooner has this brave and straightforward man passed these tests than he is told of the slaughter of his wife and children. Their death is the price he has paid for flying to England to seek Malcolm's return and his country's safety.

At first the news of this mass murder seems to crush Macduff and we feel for him deeply. He has suffered a hideous injustice. Simultaneously we see the full measure of Macbeth's evil and, as Macduff painfully turns his anguish into thoughts of revenge, the glimmering of a real hope for Scotland. In Act IV Scene iii Macduff is tested to the absolute. Because of our sympathy for him we begin to feel the very real good that Malcolm and his forces can bring to Scotland. We want them to win now and we want Macduff to have his chance of single combat with Macbeth.

It is Macduff, fighting both for his country and his own revenge, who gives the order for battle (V, vi). Now, as the English forces start to win, Macduff resolves either to fight Macbeth or no one ('. . . else my sword with an unbattered edge/I sheathe again undeeded'). We watch his meeting with Macbeth and watch the fight between the two men. Macduff is Macbeth's last and most telling cause for despair; he understands the hatred Macduff has for him and he has purposely sought to avoid fighting him. Now he is challenged by him and he tells Macduff of one of the last of the Witches' prophecies, of their so-called promises of Macbeth's well-being:

> *I bear a charmèd life, which must not yield*
> *To one of woman born.*

(V, vi, ll. 51–2)

Macduff then explains the nature of his birth: a Caesarean section. He was not born by the efforts of a woman but was from his 'mother's womb/Untimely ripped'. This destroys Macbeth's last hope. It is this truth that forces him to acknowledge that the Witches 'palter with us in a double sense' and so have led him to his damnation. Macbeth refuses to fight. He is told by Macduff that he will be publicly humiliated if he surrenders. The last shreds of Macbeth's courage are gathered up and he fights until his eventual and inevitable defeat. Macduff is now the good, the brave man of action. By decapitating Macbeth the traitor, he takes over the role played by Macbeth at the start of the play, when he cut off Macdonwald's head: Macduff is the trusted and loyal man of action in the service of his rightful king.

DUNCAN

The personality of Duncan is less important than his role: he is the rightful king appointed by God (see 'The Nature of Kingship', pp. 80–82). He is a big-hearted and generous man, quick to reward and praise but also quick to punish. He is a strong man and, more importantly, a very good man. Macbeth knows (I, vii) that Duncan's virtues will make the condemnation of his murder, 'the deep damnation of his taking-off', even more bitter. Macduff, while being tested by Malcolm (IV, iii, l. 109) calls Duncan 'a most sainted king'. All these virtues – holiness, generosity and a sense of justice – are the attributes of a good king. The absence of them in Macbeth points to his tyrannous nature.

MALCOLM

Malcolm is the murdered Duncan's rightful heir. To make this point clear we see Malcolm named as heir immediately after the battle in the first Act. It is only after the murder, however, that we see Malcolm growing in stature. We watch the emergence of a very shrewd young man.

The practical side of Malcolm's nature is demonstrated as soon as the murder has taken place (II, iii). Malcolm realizes that it is dangerous for him to stay in Scotland and, to avoid repercussions, he steals away to England. There, because he is the true heir, he is received by the pious Edward the Confessor with great 'grace'. It is right that Malcolm should be in England; by being associated with Edward the Confessor, he will also be associated with true kingship at its very finest (see 'The Nature of Kingship', pp. 80–82). This emphasizes the idea of Malcolm's virtue when he finally returns to Scotland.

But natural goodness is not sufficient for a king: he must be a realist. That Malcolm is so comes across most clearly in Act IV Scene iii. In his handling of Macduff – the test to discover whether he is a double agent – we see this very clearly. Malcolm is not to be easily deceived. When, for the good of Scotland, he gently but persistently tries to convert Macduff's grief into positive revenge, we see Malcolm as a wise, able and shrewd young man.

And Malcolm's youth is important. It seems to bring with it the promise of hope. This is in marked contrast to Macbeth's pessimism, his readiness for death in Act V. At the end of the play, Malcolm takes on the role of his country's doctor. He is the skilful surgeon come to cure Scotland. It is he who orders his soldiers to camouflage themselves with the boughs from Birnam Wood; he thereby fulfils the prophecy and so shakes Macbeth's confidence in the Witches. Malcolm's victory over Macbeth is a relatively easy one, but his final speech at the end of the play shows him to be at once young, efficient and good. His coronation restores peace, truth and legitimate kingship to Scotland.

Commentary

You should remember that *Macbeth* was first performed in 1606, well over three and a half centuries ago. People then had a number of ideas about the world that were very different from our own. You should try to have a sympathetic appreciation of these if you want to understand Shakespeare's world and Shakespeare's play.

THE NATURE OF KINGSHIP

Perhaps the most important of these ideas is the nature of kingship. England is now ruled by a constitutional monarchy. This means that the Queen is a figurehead and that real power is invested in Parliament. This was less true in Shakespeare's day, and *Macbeth* deliberately heightens some of the ideas about monarchy held by his patron, James I.

The most important notion to grasp is that it was believed that kings were ultimately appointed by God and were responsible for preserving the good and natural order of things in the lands over which they ruled. It is because Duncan had this direct authority from God (he and his family having been chosen as rulers of Scotland) that Macbeth and his wife are wary of committing murder, and, as they think about doing so, summon up images of night, of heaven blacked out and the murder taking place unseen:

> *Come, thick night,*
> *And pall thee in the dunnest smoke of hell,*
> *That my keen knife see not the wound it makes,*

> *Nor heaven peep through the blanket of the dark*
> *To cry, 'Hold, hold!'*

> (I, v, ll. 48–52)

It is not mere physical cowardice that restrains Macbeth. He is a brave soldier. What frightens him is the knowledge that to kill his king will cut him off from God, from all that is good. He will destroy the natural order of things created by God and preserved through the King. His punishment for this will be the inability to pray or sleep, and the endless and ever more bloody action he will have to undertake in the vain hope of making himself secure. It is these deeds: the murder of Banquo, of Lady Macduff and the hundred others that Ross reports (IV, iii, ll. 164–73), that will exhaust him and lead to his destruction – a destruction he has brought upon himself by the murder of Duncan.

We are twice told that Duncan is a good and a holy man. The first time Macbeth himself tells us this; the second time, Macduff (IV, iii, ll. 108–9). This is true; but such piety does not in itself account for the deepest layer of evil in the murder. It is, to repeat, the fact that Duncan is king that matters. Shakespeare's audience, of course, would have been more familiar with this idea than we are; but, just to underline the theme of the holiness and the special nature of kingship, *Macbeth* tells us a great deal about another great and pious king: Edward the Confessor.

In a brief interlude in Act IV Scene iii, Malcolm describes the practice of 'touching for the King's Evil'. It was believed at this time that the kings of England had been given the power by God to cure a disfiguring disease called scrofula. This miracle-working ability (Malcolm himself calls it 'miraculous') was a special sign of God's favour; of the English king's powers being greater than those of ordinary mortals. Edward has other gifts:

> *With this strange virtue*
> *He hath a heavenly gift of prophecy,*
> *And sundry blessings hang about his throne*
> *That speak him full of grace.*

> (IV, iii, ll. 156–9)

Thus Edward is a prophet and a man specially favoured by God. This atmosphere of blessedness is important. It enhances Malcolm's prestige as the rightful king of Scotland that he is welcomed in such a court and, when he marches with the English forces to reclaim his throne, we are led to believe that a special aura of holiness does indeed surround a monarch.

This is in sharp distinction to Macbeth. It is important to note that he is referred to as the 'tyrant'. Macbeth has the worldly power of a king which he has seized by worldly means. No special grace invests his throne. Rather, the evil aura of the Witches brings with it violence, bloodshed and despair. True kings – Duncan, Malcolm, Edward the Confessor – bring peace to their countries because they rule through God's grace and are fine men. The self-made king, the tyrant Macbeth, has upset the natural order of things and can only bring destruction to Scotland and eventually to himself. He is replaced by Malcolm because, in the end, it is shown that his evil is self-destructive – the second great theme of the play.

THE NATURE OF EVIL

On the first occasion Macbeth meets the Witches (I, iii) he asks them the source of their power and why they have singled him out:

> *Say from whence*
> *You owe this strange intelligence; or why*
> *Upon this blasted heath you stop our way*
> *With such prophetic greeting? Speak, I charge you!*
>
> (I, iii, ll. 74–7)

The stage direction that immediately follows is very simple: *Witches vanish.* They will neither receive orders from mortals nor will they say where they come from or explain their actions. The origins of their evil remain a mystery.

Rather than trying to explain where the Witches come from (a question left unanswered and so all the more mysterious), Shakespeare has a greater interest in showing how evil works.

The central point to grasp here is that the Witches *do* very little. They appear, they tell the truth and their prophecies are always fulfilled by men. The Witches tell Macbeth that he is going to be the Thane of Cawdor and King of Scotland. Almost as soon as they disappear Ross and Angus tell him that King Duncan has created Macbeth Thane of Cawdor in return for his loyalty and bravery in battle. Macbeth is thunderstruck. The Witches have told him two things that appeal to his ambition. The first of these is at once fulfilled. Clearly, as Macbeth later writes to his wife: 'they have more in them than mortal knowledge'. He believes them: partly because they seem to speak the truth and partly because they tell him things he wants to hear. It is important to notice that Macbeth ignores Banquo's crucial warning:

> ... *oftentimes, to win us to our harm,*
> *The instruments of darkness tell us truths;*
> *Win us with honest trifles, to betray's*
> *In deepest consequence.*

(I, iii, ll. 122–5).

This is what will happen. We do not see the Witches again until Act III Scene v, and they do not meet Macbeth again until Act IV Scene i. By this time Macbeth has murdered Duncan, murdered the two grooms, been crowned in Scotland, had Banquo killed and been visited by Banquo's ghost. He is a man on the perilous edge of insanity.

He knows perfectly well that it is wrong to murder Duncan. As soon as the Witches have spoken to him we see him plunged in thought, their words sinking down through the layers of his mind and his imagination. When he breaks into soliloquy it is to express horror at the thought of murdering his king:

> ... *why do I yield to that suggestion*
> *Whose horrid image doth unfix my hair,*
> *And make my seated heart knock at my ribs*
> *Against the use of nature?*

(I, iii, ll. 133–6)

He *has* thought of murder, and until Duncan is dead we shall see him wrestling with almost unbearable temptation.

At first he hopes he can leave it all to chance, but with the entry of Lady Macbeth such thoughts are useless. Macbeth knows the horror to which the murder will expose him. Lady Macbeth believes that power can be seized by an effort of will and by ignoring natural promptings of conscience. For her these are weaknesses, unmanly things. By telling Macbeth that he is weak and unmanly and by convincing him that they will never be caught, she wins him over. Lady Macbeth tries to personify strength and evil. By doing this she converts Macbeth to evil. She goads him, she taunts him, and he gives in to the temptation for the sake of power.

In being led into temptation, Macbeth has wrought his nerves to a high pitch. Act I Scene vii illustrates this. Then in Act II Scene i, as he is preparing to steal to Duncan's bedroom, he sees the vision of the dagger. The great man of action reported to us in the battle is now a quivering mass of murderous ambition. The power of this ambition is so great, however, that Macbeth finds the willpower to kill his king. All that was good about him has now been perverted. As he returns from the murder chamber he is a man in anguish. From now on he can neither pray nor sleep. The result of his evil is utter anguish. This is how evil works the self-destruction of evil-doers.

Despite Lady Macbeth's magnificent appearance of evil strength, people cannot merely will themselves into being wicked and then hope to shrug off the consequences. Conscience, human feelings – these are real powers. For all her bravado, Lady Macbeth cannot murder Duncan when it comes to the point, because he looks like her father.

For Macbeth and his wife, their crime will bring them a life ever more intolerably stressful. They will put a brave face on things, but they will learn that they are not safe, secure, happy. Lady Macbeth breaks out pathetically:

> *Naught's had, all's spent,*
> *Where our desire is got without content.*
> *'Tis safer to be that which we destroy*
> *Than by destruction dwell in doubtful joy.*

(III, ii, ll. 4–7)

Macbeth, too, is being worn down by the effects of his own evil. He realizes that Banquo must be destroyed: first because he suspects Macbeth and, secondly, because it was prophesied that his descendants would be kings. If this comes about, then Macbeth has murdered and sold his soul for no reward. He is deeply embroiled in his wickedness but he thinks he can escape from its consequences, that he is still master of his fate. He is not. He has no control over the forces of evil, though he will try to murder his way to safety. He wrongly believes that 'things bad begun make strong themselves by ill': in other words, he thinks that two wrongs will make a right.

The murder of Banquo only furthers the self-destructive energies of evil. Banquo's ghost returns to haunt Macbeth, who is driven almost mad by panic. His wife, too, is destroyed by the strain of trying to keep up appearances. We see her exhausted at the end of the haunted feast; we do not see her again until the beginning of Act V when she is a broken, mad woman. She has urged evil upon Macbeth and the strain of the consequences has driven her insane. At the start of the play she was the woman who believed she could do anything without fear. Now, at the close, her conscience has wholly overcome her. Again, evil is self-destructive.

Macbeth is made of similar but stronger stuff. After the banquet scene he goes to the Witches once more, little knowing that they have agreed on his destruction, agreed to drive him beyond commonsense 'security' so that he too will be all but mad. In this second meeting Macbeth learns that he is right to be suspicious of Macduff, that he need not fear until Birnam Wood marches against his castle and he confronts a man not naturally born of woman. He is then shown to 'grieve his heart' that Banquo's children will indeed inherit the throne of Scotland. In his despair, Macbeth lashes out against Macduff's family in a demented and barbarous way. But, with his growing desperation and violence, and his despairing exhaustion, we see the forces of good gathering strength. These *are* more powerful than evil. One by one the charms of the Witches, once interpreted as pledges of safety, are shown to be false. Macbeth confronts Macduff without any confidence in the magic charms. Barely caring whether he lives or dies, he summons the strength to fight and is killed. Good, personified in Malcolm and Macduff, is a real and positive force. Evil, personified in Macbeth and his wife, can only wear itself out to the point of final defeat. Malcolm wins, good wins, and Macbeth and his wife are finally no more than 'this dead butcher and his fiend-like queen'.

Examination Questions

1. Read the following passage, and answer all the questions printed beneath it:

```
BANQUO                What are these
   So withered and so wild in their attire,
   That look not like the inhabitants o' the earth,
   And yet are on't? Live you? Or are you aught
   That man may question? You seem to understand me      5
   By each at once her choppy finger laying
   Upon her skinny lips. You should be women;
   And yet your beards forbid me to interpret
   That you are so.
MACBETH              Speak if you can! What are you?
FIRST WITCH All hail, Macbeth! Hail to thee, Thane of Glamis!   10
SECOND WITCH All hail, Macbeth! Hail to thee, Thane of
   Cawdor!
THIRD WITCH All hail, Macbeth, that shalt be king hereafter!
BANQUO Good sir, why do you start, and seem to fear
   Things that do sound so fair? – I' the name of truth,
   Are ye fantastical, or that indeed                   15
   Which outwardly ye show? My noble partner
   You greet with present grace, and great prediction
   Of noble having and of royal hope
   That he seems rapt withal. To me you speak not.
   If you can look into the seeds of time              20
   And say which grain will grow and which will not,
   Speak then to me, who neither beg nor fear
   Your favours nor your hate.
```

FIRST WITCH Hail!
SECOND WITCH Hail!   25
THIRD WITCH Hail!
FIRST WITCH Lesser than Macbeth, and greater.
SECOND WITCH Not so happy, yet much happier.
THIRD WITCH Thou shalt get kings, though thou be none.
  So, all hail, Macbeth and Banquo!   30
FIRST WITCH Banquo and Macbeth, all hail!
MACBETH Stay, you imperfect speakers! Tell me more!
  By Sinell's death I know I am Thane of Glamis;
  But how of Cawdor? The Thane of Cawdor lives
  A prosperous gentleman. And to be king   35
  Stands not within the prospect of belief –
  No more than to be Cawdor. Say from whence
  You owe this strange intelligence; or why
  Upon this blasted heath you stop our way
  With such prophetic greeting? Speak, I charge you!   40

(i) Bring out in your own words the meaning of lines 16–19 (*My noble partner . . . rapt withal*).

(ii) *the Thane of Cawdor lives/A prosperous gentleman* (lines 34–5). What is Macbeth soon to learn about Cawdor?

(iii) Bring out the contrast in the reactions of Banquo and Macbeth to the witches.

        (*University of Oxford Local Examination Board, 1979*)

2. Taking care to support your opinion by as much evidence as you can find in speeches and episodes in the play, discuss

(*a*) Macbeth's attitude to the murder of Duncan *before* the deed was committed, *and*

(*b*) the other principal factors that spurred Macbeth on to committing the murder.

3. Choose *two* scenes (or parts of scenes) from the play which seem

to you to be particularly full of horror, and *one* scene (or part of a scene) which seems to you to contain humour *or* pathos. Describe each part of the play that you select, making clear by quotation or close reference what you consider makes it full of horror, or gives it the quality of humour or pathos.

(*University of London Examination Board, 1970*)

4. Read the following passage and answer the questions below it.

LADY MACBETH Glamis thou art, and Cawdor; and shalt be
  What thou art promised. Yet do I fear thy nature:
  It is too full o' the milk of human-kindness
  To catch the nearest way. Thou wouldst be great,
  Art not without ambition, but without   5
  The illness should attend it. What thou wouldst highly
  That wouldst thou holily, wouldst not play false,
  And yet wouldst wrongly win. Thou'dst have, great Glamis,
  That which cries, 'Thus must thou do' if thou have it,
  And that which rather thou dost fear to do   10
  Than wishest should be undone. Hie thee hither
  That I may pour my spirits in thine ear,
  And chastise with the valour of my tongue
  All that impedes thee from the golden round
  Which fate and metaphysical aid doth seem   15
  To have thee crowned withal.

      Enter a Messenger

                What is your tidings?

MESSENGER The King comes here tonight.
LADY MACBETH   Thou'rt mad to say it!
  Is not thy master with him? Who, were't so,   20
  Would have informed for preparation.
MESSENGER So please you, it is true. Our Thane is coming;
  One of my fellows had the speed of him,

Who, almost dead for breath, had scarcely more
Than would make up his message.   25
LADY MACBETH   Give him tending;
He brings great news.

(*a*) Give, in your own words, the contents of the letter Lady Macbeth has just received.

(*b*) This is Lady Macbeth's first appearance in the play. What impression of her personality do you gain from this passage?

(*c*) Express, in your own words, Lady Macbeth's opinion of her husband as shown in this passage.

(*d*) Give an account, in your own words, of her first conversation with her husband.

5. Referring to the actions and speeches of Macbeth and Banquo up to the time of Macbeth's first appearance as king, contrast their responses to their meeting with the Witches and make clear what aspects of their characters are shown.

(*University of London Examination Board, 1972*)

6. Read the following passage and answer the questions below it.

LADY MACBETH That which hath made them drunk hath
    made me bold;
What hath quenched them hath given me fire.
    – Hark! – Peace!
It was the owl that shrieked, the fatal bellman,
Which gives the stern'st good-night. He is about it.
The doors are open, and the surfeited grooms
Do mock their charge with snores; I have drugged their
    possets
That death and nature do contend about them
Whether they live or die.
MACBETH [*within*]   Who's there? What, ho!

LADY MACBETH Alack! I am afraid they have awaked,
And 'tis not done. The attempt and not the deed
Confounds us. – Hark! – I laid their daggers ready;
He could not miss 'em. Had he not resembled
My father as he slept, I had done't.

Enter Macbeth carrying two bloodstained daggers

My husband!
MACBETH I have done the deed. Didst thou not hear a noise?
LADY MACBETH I heard the owl-scream and the cricket's cry.
Did not you speak?
MACBETH When?
LADY MACBETH Now.
MACBETH As I descended?
LADY MACBETH Ay.
MACBETH Hark!
Who lies i' the second chamber?
LADY MACBETH Donalbain.
MACBETH (*looks at his hands*) This is a sorry sight.
LADY MACBETH A foolish thought, to say a sorry sight.
MACBETH There's one did laugh in's sleep, and one cried
'Murder!'
That they did wake each other. I stood and heard them.
But they did say their prayers, and addressed them
Again to sleep.
LADY MACBETH There are two lodged together.
MACBETH One cried 'God bless us' and 'Amen' the other,
As they had seen me with these hangman's hands.
Listening their fear, I could not say 'Amen'
When they did say 'God bless us.'
LADY MACBETH Consider it not so deeply.
MACBETH But wherefore could not I pronounce 'Amen'?
I had most need of blessing, and 'Amen'
Stuck in my throat.
LADY MACBETH These deeds must not be thought
After these ways; so, it will make us mad.

(*a*) Show how this passage creates a mood of suspense and horror.

(*b*) 'Had he not resembled/My father as he slept, I had done't.' Contrast this statement with one made earlier in the play by Lady Macbeth in which she expresses very different sentiments, and comment on the contrast.

(*c*) Write a brief account of the remainder of the scene from which the passage is taken.

7. 'The world of the play is not entirely evil.' What have you found in the speeches and actions of the characters to support this view?

8. 'Fair is foul and foul is fair.' By close reference to *three* episodes in the play, show how Shakespeare reveals events and characters as not being what they seem.

(*University of London Examination Board, 1973*)

9. Write an account of the scene set in England, and show what its main purpose is in the development of the play.

10. At the end of the play Malcolm describes Lady Macbeth as 'fiend-like'. By reference to her speeches and actions throughout the play, show how far you agree with this judgement.

(*University of London Examination Board, 1974*)

11. Read the following passage, and answer all the questions printed beneath it:

MACBETH If it were done when 'tis done, then 'twere well
  It were done quickly. If the assassination
  Could trammel up the consequence, and catch
  With his surcease success – that but this blow

Might be the be-all and the end-all – here,   5
But here, upon this bank and shoal of time,
We'd jump the life to come. But in these cases
We still have judgment here – that we but teach
Bloody instructions, which, being taught, return
To plague the inventor. This even-handed justice   10
Commends the ingredients of our poisoned chalice
To our own lips. He's here in double trust:
First, as I am his kinsman and his subject,
Strong both against the deed; then, as his host,
Who should against his murderer shut the door,   15
Not bear the knife myself. Besides, this Duncan
Hath borne his faculties so meek, hath been
So clear in his great office, that his virtues
Will plead like angels trumpet-tongued against
The deep damnation of his taking-off;   20
And Pity, like a naked new-born babe
Striding the blast, or heaven's cherubin, horsed
Upon the sightless curriers of the air,
Shall blow the horrid deed in every eye,
That tears shall drown the wind. I have no spur   25
To prick the sides of my intent but only
Vaulting ambition which o'erleaps itself
And falls on the other.

(i) Bring in your own words the sense of lines 2–4 (*if the assassination ... success*); and lines 25–6 (*I have no ... my intent*).

(ii) Pick out from this passage two examples of vivid language, and say why you find them striking.

(iii) What do you learn from this passage of Macbeth's conflicting emotions?

12. Read the following passage, and answer all the questions printed beneath it:

GENTLEWOMAN It is an accustomed action with her to seem

thus washing her hands. I have known her to continue in
this a quarter of an hour.

LADY MACBETH Yet here's a spot.

DOCTOR Hark! she speaks. I will set down what comes from 5
her, to satisfy my remembrance the more strongly.

LADY MACBETH Out, damned spot! Out, I say! One: two: why,
then, 'tis time to do 't. — Hell is murky! — Fie, my lord, fie!
A soldier, and afeard? — What need we fear who knows it,
when none can call our power to accompt? — Yet who 10
would have thought the old man to have had so much
blood in him?

DOCTOR Do you mark that?

LADY MACBETH The Thane of Fife had a wife: where is she
now? — What, will these hands ne'er be clean? — No more o' 15
that, my lord, no more o' that. You mar all with this starting.

DOCTOR Go to, go to; you have known what you should not.

GENTLEWOMAN She has spoke what she should not, I am
sure of that: Heaven knows what she has known.

LADY MACBETH Here's the smell of the blood still. All the 20
perfumes of Arabia will not sweeten this little hand. Oh!
Oh! Oh!

DOCTOR What a sigh is there! The heart is sorely charged.

GENTLEWOMAN I would not have such a heart in my bosom
for the dignity of the whole body. 25

(i) Give in your own words the meaning of line 16 (*You mar all
with this starting*), and line 23 (*The heart is sorely charged*).

(ii) Describe precisely Lady Macbeth's state of mind at this point
in the play.

(iii) Explain carefully what events Lady Macbeth is recalling in this
passage.

13. Either, (*a*) Give an account of the scene (IV, ii) in which Lady
Macduff is murdered.

Or, (*b*) Which character in *Macbeth*, other than Macbeth or Lady
Macbeth, has contributed the most to your interest in the play?

Or, (*c*) Discuss the importance of the supernatural in *Macbeth*.
(*University of Oxford Local Examination Board, 1979*)

14. Read the following passage, and answer all the questions printed beneath it:

MACBETH   This push
  Will cheer me ever or dis-seat me now.
  I have liv'd long enough: my way of life
  Is fallen into the sere, the yellow leaf;
  And that which should accompany old age,   5
  As honour, love, obedience, troops of friends,
  I must not look to have; but, in their stead,
  Curses, not loud, but deep, mouth-honour, breath,
  Which the poor heart would fain deny, and dare not. –
  Seyton!   10

Enter SEYTON.

SEYTON What's your gracious pleasure?
MACBETH   What news more?
SEYTON All is confirmed, my lord, which was reported.
MACBETH I'll fight till from my bones my flesh be hacked.
  Give me my armour.
SEYTON   'Tis not needed yet.
MACBETH I'll put it on.   15
  Send out more horses, skirr the country round,
  Hang those that talk of fear. – Give me mine armour. –
  How does your patient, doctor?
DOCTOR   Not so sick, my lord,
  As she is troubled with thick-coming fancies
  That keep her from her rest.
MACBETH   Cure her of that.   20
  Canst thou not minister to a mind diseased,
  Pluck from the memory a rooted sorrow,
  Raze out the written troubles of the brain,

And with some sweet oblivious antidote
Cleanse the stuffed bosom of that perilous stuff   25
Which weighs upon the heart?

(i) Bring out in your own words the meaning of lines 1–4
(*This push ... yellow leaf*).

(ii) *All is confirmed, my lord, which was reported* (line 12).
State precisely what had been reported.

(iii) What do you learn about Macbeth from this passage?

15. Either, (*a*) Give an account of the scene (IV, i) in which
Macbeth visits the Witches.

Or, (*b*) Give a careful account of what the Porter says and
does in the scene in which he appears. What does he contribute
to the interest of the play?

Or, (*c*) 'We can have no sympathy for her.' Discuss this
judgement on Lady Macbeth.

(*University of Oxford Local Examination Board, 1979*)

16. Read the following passage and answer all the questions
printed beneath it:

LADY MACBETH Yet here's a spot.

DOCTOR Hark! She speaks. I will set down what comes from
  her, to satisfy my remembrance the more strongly.

LADY MACBETH Out, damned spot! Out, I say! – One: two:
  why, then, 'tis time to do't. – Hell is murky! – Fie, my lord,   5
  fie! A soldier and afeard? – What need we fear who knows it,
  when none can call our power to accompt? Yet who
  would have thought the old man to have had so much
  blood in him?

DOCTOR Do you mark that?   10

LADY MACBETH The Thane of Fife had a wife; where is she
  now? – What, will these hands ne'er be clean? – No more

o' that, my lord, no more o' that. You mar all with this
starting.

DOCTOR   Go to, go to: you have known what you should not.   15

GENTLEWOMAN   She has spoke what she should not, I am
sure of that. Heaven knows what she has known.

LADY MACBETH   Here's the smell of the blood still. All the
perfumes of Arabia will not sweeten this little hand. Oh!
Oh! Oh!   20

DOCTOR   What a sigh is there! The heart is sorely charged.

GENTLEWOMAN   I would not have such a heart in my bosom
for the dignity of the whole body.

DOCTOR   Well, well, well.

GENTLEWOMAN   Pray God it be, sir.   25

DOCTOR   This disease is beyond my practice; yet I have known
those which have walked in their sleep who have died holily
in their beds.

LADY MACBETH   Wash your hands; put on your nightgown;
look not so pale. I tell you yet again, Banquo's buried; he   30
cannot come out on's grave.

DOCTOR   Even so?

LADY MACBETH   To bed, to bed! There's knocking at the gate.
Come, come, come, come, give me your hand. What's done
cannot be undone. To bed, to bed, to bed.   [*Exit.*   35

(i)   Explain *when none can ... to accompt* (lines 6–7); *you mar ... this
starting* (line 13); *the dignity of the whole body* (line 23).

(ii)   At this stage of the play, what has Lady Macbeth commanded
to have continually beside her at night? Why does she need it?

(iii)   How is Lady Macbeth's disturbed state of mind conveyed here,
and how are we reminded of the causes of this disturbance?

(*University of Oxford Local Examination Board, 1983*)